# WAYMAN WILLS AND ADMINISTRATIONS

PRESERVED IN THE

## PREROGATIVE COURT OF CANTERBURY,

1383—1821.

BY

### J. HARVEY BLOOM, M.A., F.S.G.

AUTHOR OF "THE GRIFFINS OF DINGLEY,"
"PEDIGREES OF THE FAMILY OF BOURNE," ETC., ETC.

Copyright © 2013 Read Books Ltd.
This book is copyright and may not be
reproduced or copied in any way without
the express permission of the publisher in writing

British Library Cataloguing-in-Publication Data
A catalogue record for this book is available from the
British Library

# James Harvey Bloom

James Harvey Bloom was an English clergyman and antiquary, born on 28th December 1860. Bloom was the son of Reverend James Graver Bloom.

He attended the University of Cambridge as a non-collegiate student, and gained his Bachelor of Arts in 1887, and his Master of Arts in 1891. After these studies, he was ordained a deacon in Calcutta (now Kolkata), the capital of the Indian state of West Bengal. Bloom then moved on to become curate of St. Andrews parish, in Hertford, England - and was curate of Hemsworth, a small town and civil parish on the edge of West Yorkshire.

Bloom soon tired of the purely ecclesiastical life however, and became Headmaster of Long Marston Grammar School from 1893 to 1895. After this, he returned to the vicarage and served as Rector of Whitchurch, Warwickshire, from 1896 to 1917. Bloom had many hobbies and interests in his private and professional life, and produced several works as a genealogist and antiquarian, including *Shakespeare's Church; An Architectural and Ecclesiastical History of the Fabric and its Ornaments* (1902), *Shakespeare's Garden* (1903), *English Seals* (1906), *English Tracts, Pamphlets and Printed Sheets* (1923), *Folklore in Shakespeare Land* (1929) and the voluminous *Medical Practitioners in the Diocese of London, 1529-1725* (1935).

Bloom died in 1944, after which all his books and works were sold at auction. His daughter was the novelist Ursula

Bloom (a prolific author who wrote her first book at the age of seven!) – she published a memoir of her father, *Parson Extraordinary*, which was published in 1963.

# CONTENTS.

|  | PAGE |
|---|---|
| Introduction | v |
| Wills | 1 |
| Administrations | 68 |
| Glossary | 75 |
| Index | 77 |

# INTRODUCTION.

The essence of a will is said to be threefold, namely: The testament (1) can be set aside or revoked; (2) It can affect property not in possession of the testator at the date of execution, but acquired before death; (3) It can make a representative to act for the testator when he is dead. In the twelfth century a man could not give away his freehold land by will; it was not so allowed until 1540. Even then the lawyers held that it could only affect land that was in the testator's possession when his will was made, and this remained good law until 1837; but in any case the will was revocable. It had no action until its owner died. The English will is the old Saxon Cwide. In the oldest form there was no expressed difficulty in a man giving something at the moment of writing, yet retaining possession for life. He could both give away and keep his land. Later it became impossible, since no gift took effect without delivery (seisin). This ancient doctrine is known as the post-obit gift. The second important characteristic of a will was the death-bed confession. Confession consists of three stages: contrition, the actual act of confession, and the amendment. The real purport of many of the clauses in early wills appears to be an endeavour to satisfy the priest of the dying man's real earnestness about his amendment. This amendment is in practice the undoing as far as may be of wrongs done. To this end he leaves sums for tithes forgotten, something towards the repair of the church and other like pious purposes, something for Masses for his soul.

It matters little whether or no these gifts are revocable and ambulatory, since it very rarely happens in practice that a man will recover after he has received *Viaticum*. Through these gifts executorship arose. The dying man is handing over to some other person certain property for the good of his soul. In the Anglo-Saxon Cwide (*i.e.*, a saying) the post-obit gift and the last words coalesce, and have much the appearance of a more modern will. The testator provides for his kinsfolk and remembers his dependants, but it shews scarce a sign of its revocable character, or its power to give what its owner may possess in the future but does not possess at the moment. Moreover, the consent of the King was necessary and a heriot had to be paid. Growth was slow and changes very gradual. They were brought about by the following alterations made in the twelfth and thirteenth centuries. (1) The King's Court condemned the post-obit gift and all dealings in land, except in certain boroughs. (2) The claim of primogeniture became arbitrary; the heir as such has nothing to do with the chattels of the dead man, which become generally the spoil of the church. (3) The church asserted her right to protect and execute the last will, and under her sway the will becomes, through foreign influence, a real testament, and the executor the dead man's representative. At length the church asserts its right to administer the dead man's goods for the welfare of his soul.

By the twelfth century a wide gulf lay between land and chattels. The land went to the heir. The lawyers of the ages of Henry II. and III. (Glanville and Bracton) allowed the church to obtain control of what was becoming a real testament, and from henceforth the Courts Christian saw to the will, and this will had executors. These were, in origin, neither Roman or English. The heir is useful. He is bound to see the executor pay the legacies; for a time he looks after the land. The executor attends to the chattels, but at the end of the Middle Ages the old Roman *heres* is called in England the executor. In the thirteenth century wills are usually in Latin, then in French, and in the second half of the fourteenth century English wills appear. The forms are *Lego, Jeo devise*, or I wyte or bequeath. The Anathema has long since passed away, but the testator's first care is not his estate, but his immortal soul and his earthly body. His soul he bequeaths to God, our Lady, and the Holy Saints. His body he gives, with a mortuary, to some church. For a long time elaborate instructions for splendid ceremonies are the rule, later the faces of the testators are set against idle pomp. Then come numerous monetary and other legacies, mostly left to pious uses, the four orders of friars, the prisons of London, the Mother Church. The repair of roads and bridges are rarely forgotten. The testator dismisses his debts and the sums owing to him with scarce a word. The later the will the more care to provide for his wife and children; the earlier it is the more the dead's part appears. He may be in sore need of Masses for his soul. A common form survives, he is "sick in body but whole in mind"—a survival this of the dying confession. Over and above the executors, powerful friends are asked to be overseers, who are to advise or assist the executor. Elaborate directions, save only for the funeral rites, are rare, and even after the Reformation much of the mediæval spirit has been preserved.

A word about probate. It was not until the age of Ranulph Glanville (*temp*. Hen. II.) that the Church Courts obtained control of wills. They then began to claim competence not only to decide the validity but also the power to establish it. By the thirteenth century wills were proved in the Church Courts. This idea in common with that of the executors came from abroad, and such claims to probate led to many an unseemly quarrel. For instance, Archbishop Peckham excommunicated the Bishop of Hereford for denying his jurisdiction in a case where the dead man had goods in more than one diocese. The compromise that a prerogative probate could only be rightly claimed when the deceased had more than the worth of five pounds in each of two dioceses is not very ancient.

It is necessary to a correct understanding to briefly state the procedure following upon the dying confession. After absolution, when the sick man was *in extremis*, the last rites of the church were administered. During his last moments the "passing bell" was tolled, and directly after his decease a solemn commendation of his soul to God followed. The death bell was then rung, the strokes indicating the age and sex of the departed. Commendation of the departed was followed by a Litany and prayer for the repose of his soul, recited either in the death chamber or the hall of his dwelling. On the evening before the funeral Vespers for the dead were recited. This office was generally known as *placebo*, from the first word of the Antiphon: I shall please the Lord in the land of the living (Ps. cxvi. 9). The service was said or sung after the body had been placed before some side altar in the parish church, where it lay covered with a pall and surrounded by six or eight wax lights.

On the following morning at service of Matins, the *Dirige*, so called from the Antiphon, Make thy way plain before my face (Ps. v. 8), was rendered in like manner. The bells of the church were tolled before the funeral, which took place after the Requiem Mass had been sung. The inhumation followed. It was succeeded by a final peal on the bells. The Trental or Month's Mind then began, and its Masses followed thirty consecutive days. Finally, the obit and anniversary with special Masses were said monthly and yearly.

A study of the following wills shews the prescribed order of services prior to the Reformation. Nor did it even then entirely cease, since communion services at funerals have never been altogether omitted in the Church of England; and in the exequies of the wealthy, especially of Peers and Prelates, there has been no lack of wax-lights and embroidered palls, bells, and other ceremonies, or in the provision of mourning for those who attended, although that attendance was no longer for the pious purpose of praying for the soul of the deceased. Recognition of the Mother Church of the Diocese died out, as of course did specified legacies to the lights of the church and the ornaments of the altars, but their place was partially taken by some small legacy to the repair of the church and for mending of highways and of bridges. At one period the pomp of post-Reformation funerals became so marked and the expense so great, that in many cases a limitation was placed upon the expenditure, and the testator desires to be buried simply—a sensible and wise provision. The attendance of a herald is now rare: hatchments are out of fashion. The bearing of the dead man's arms and banner are no more. Gradually a sane theory as to the disposal of the departed is growing in favour, though much needless expense is still incurred.

The name of Wayman in the Teutonic form Wigmund occurs in England as early as A.D. 725, in which year a prelate of that name was Abbot of Worcester; half-a-century later another Wigmund filled the See of York, and from 895—910 another was Bishop of Lichfield. The name is cognate with Wigmaer, Wymarc or Wihomarc, one of whom was Abbot of Westminster in the year 969. The name is of Scandinavian origin, and frequent not only in Norway, Sweden and Denmark, but along the coast line of the North Sea as far south as Normandy. In England the Domesday Book shews branches of the family settled in Bedfordshire, Berkshire, Essex, Herts, Oxon and Suffolk. In Fressingfield, in the last-named county, Robert, son of Wimare, held six carucates of land in the time of King Edward, while in Groton in the same county

Roger de Orber encroached upon his lands. In Lincolnshire one Wymound was an under-tenant of Count Alan, another held his land of Ivo Taillegebosc. Others of the name occur among the men of the Bishop of Bayeaux and Robert of Poitou. At Corton in Suffolk, Geoffrey Wymer held lands in the time of King John, and at Ipswich, some time later, a Wimund, son of Eadmund le Cartere, held land in the parish of St. Nicholas. At Freston in Suffolk the prior and convent of Snapes granted land by an undated charter to Wimund the chaplain. The most famous Suffolk owner of the name was Wimer the chaplain, who supervised, together with Bartholemew de Glanville and Robert de Valoynes the erection of Orford Castle, as appears by the Pipe Rolls 12—30 Hen. II., 1165—1184. During the years 1177—1179 he was sheriff of the county, and as such saw to the repair of the Castle of Eye. In the year 1201-2 he was the King's Justiciar, and died Vicar of Orford, a man of many parts. The name of Robert Wymound figures among the bailiffs of the town of Cambridge in the reigns of Henry III. and Edward I., especially from 1270—1284. Then in 1306 Adam Wymond was one of the representatives of the Borough of Orford in Parliament. A William Wymund lived in Surrey in 1317, a Nicholas Wyman at Haylesham in 1342; a John Wymer at Shottisham in Suffolk in 1318, and William Wayman occurs at Little Torrington, co. Devon, in 1257. Such notices could be largely extended. At a later date, viz., in 1526, Richard Wayman held considerable estates in the counties of Hereford and Worcester, and Thomas Wenman *alias* Wayman, Esq., possessed yet wider estates in Norfolk, Sussex and Worcester *temp.* Elizabeth. Katherine Weymond, a rich Suffolk widow, owned lands in Monks Soham, Bedfield and Wingfield, while the very early form of the name was represented in the same county by Edward Wimarke, who flourished about 1588.

# INTRODUCTION.

This summary confirms the information supplied by the following wills, and will help the student to understand the forms the name has taken. In the wills here given we meet with the following variants: Wymond, Wymonde, Wimond, Weymond, Wiyman, Wijman, Wiman, Wymant, Wymont, Wyment, Weyman, Weaman, Whayman, Wheighman, Wayman, Waymon, Wayneman, Wainman, Winman and Wenman. The various families were scattered along the coast from Yorkshire to Cornwall, penetrating inland from the fenland district through Cambridgeshire, Bedfordshire and Oxford into Berkshire. Several place names are derived from early squatters, such as Wymondham, Wymondhale, Wymondley and Wymondestane. They appear to have been an energetic race of yeomen and freeholders, though by no means neglectful of commerce, more than one wealthy merchant founding a successful business in London; and in such cases the wills, if early, are usually of much interest. One or two shew a love of books, and one at least collected botanical and natural history specimens. As a family they were unusually careless about the pronunciation and spelling of their surname, and in the dialect of East Anglia the same indifference is still to be found, the rustic speech rarely discriminating between Wayman and Wenman, using the two names synonymously.

The following wills of the Wayman family shew not only that many of the family had riches sufficient to require probate in the Archbishop's Court, but that the wills of quite humble testators, if they died on the high seas in the forces of the Crown, were also proved in the Prerogative Court. In one will at least the custom of London is followed, by which, in accordance with very ancient precedent, dating back to our Saxon forefathers, the property of the deceased was divided into three portions: the widow's part, the bairn's part, and the dead man's part.

## INTRODUCTION.

The series now printed serves a useful purpose in presenting much of interest in the manners and customs of our forefathers, and its value to genealogists and interest to members of the family are obvious. If the evil that men do lives after them, it may be as well to be reminded that there is another side to the picture—that for good or evil personality is indestructible and the human *ego* immortal. Even though dead, buried and forgotten, it influences the coming ages to the end of time, and perhaps after—who knows?

# WAYMAN WILLS IN THE PREROGATIVE COURT OF CANTERBURY.
## 1383—1821.

THOMAS WYMOND, Citizen and Fuller of London.

### 25 August 1496.

Soule to Almyghtie God my Creator and Saviour, to our Blessed Ladye Virgyne Sainte Mary and to all Saintes. Body to be buried in the parysshe church of Sainte Mary Wolnothe in Lumbartstrete as nere there as may be to the buryng place of the body of Johane late my wyfe. To the high altar for myne offerings negligently forgoten or withdrawen to the discharge of my soule vi$^s$ viii$^d$ sterlinge. Residue to Elizabeth my wyfe, she to doo and dispose of her awne free will as she thynketh best to pleas god and for the helth of my soul. She and Hugh Pemberton, Alderman of London, and Avery Rawson, citizen and mercer of London, to be Executors. My messuage in Shotborne Lane in the said parisshe to Elizabeth my wife for life, she to keep an obit within the said church of S$^t$ Mary Wolnothe. The Preestis and Clerks there to syng with note for my sowle, and that of Johan my late wife, and for all christen soules, with placebo and dirige overnight and Mass of Requiem, with lightes, Rynging of belles, and v shillings to be distributed, and to the parson of the church viii$^d$, to the parisshe preest 6$d$. and to every stipendarye present iiii and to the ij clerks likewise. In Wex for the light brennyng at the obite iiij$^d$. The Residue in brede, ale and chese. The said messuage to pass at the death of my wife to the parson and wardens of the said church to the continuance of the Fraternitye of our blessed Lady within the church, and for the masse of our Lady that it be better kept. Provided my obit be kept.

Proved at Lamehyth 18 Oct. 1496 by Elizabeth. (Horne, 3.)

EMOTE FERMER [*alias* WYNMAN] of Witteney,
co. Oxenford.

5 April 1501.

Soule unto Allmyghtie God and to oure blessed Lady and to all the Company of Heven. My body to be buried w'in the churche of Oure Lady of Witteney beforesaide, before the awter of Mary Magdaleyn by side my husbond Thomas Fermer. Modere Church of Lincoln xij$^d$. Unto the High Awter of Wytteney beforesaide iij$^s$ iiij$^d$. To the Rode Light of the saide churche iij lb. of waxe, and to every light in the saide church iij lb. wax. I bequeath to fynde a lampe by fore the Rode in the body of the churche for the terme of ij yeres xiii$^s$ iiij$^d$. To the reparacion of the belles xiij$^s$ iiij$^d$. To buye a palle otherwyse called a Canapie to the said churche iiij$li$. To the reparacoun of the saide churche xl$^s$. To the reparacōn of the parishe churche of Saint Elen in Abendon xl$^s$. To every poore man and woman in the Newe Almeshouse and the Olde Almeshouse in Abendon vij$^d$. Unto the churche of Bleebury in Barkshire xx$^s$. Unto the church of Langford xx$^s$. To the churches of Bradwell, Kelmyscote and Minster Lovell, xiij$^s$ iiij$^d$ each to bye theme vestments. To the iiij orderes of Freres in Oxenford x$^s$ each. My eldest son Richard Wynman 100$li$. My 2$^{nd}$ son John Wynman 100$li$. and a house in the Highe St. of Wytteney, below that of W$^m$ Fermer on the north side. Son William Fermer 100$li$. and house and land in the tithing of Hayley, and a house in Witteney, and all the Imparall of the Halle, the parlour, and the great chamber. To my son Richard Fermer all my lands in Chadlington West End, and lands in Wittney, except that bequeathed to John Wyman, and that S$^r$ John Whitting dwellith in. To said Richard Fermer all my land in Clanfelde, Benhey and Westweld. John Hewys my son in law xx$^s$. To Alice Hewes my doughter x marc. To Richard her son xl$^s$. My cousin Thomas Barett xx$^s$ and vi spones. To my da. Alice Wennam xl$^s$, and to Anne her da. v$li$., and to Emote, Kateryn and Thomas, her children, xl$^s$ and a masser, sum vi$li$. and iij massers. To Joane da. of Laurens Fermer x marc and to Thomas his younger son xl$^s$. To John Whiting my prest x$^s$ and the house that he dwellith in w$^t$ di acr. arrabull lande t'me of his life, and after his discease to remayne unto John Welyms and John Wheler and their heirs. To Elizabeth Dawson xx$^s$. To John Dawson x$^s$ and a cowe, a yewe and a lambe. To John Fermer xx$^s$. To Thomas Streche xx$^s$ and a cowe. To Elizabeth Hikman, my servant, xl$^s$, a brass pott and ij todde of myddull wolle. To my servant Milsent xx$^s$, a brasse potte and a todde of myddull wolle. To my servant Alice Heritage xx$^s$, a brasse potte and wolle. To every my god children w$^t$in the parish and w$^t$out a yewe and a lambe. To the reparacon of the newe brigge of Stanlake iiij$li$. I will that my executors spende at my burying and monthe mynde for the welth of my soule 100 mares, and every yere followyng of xxx yeres xx$^s$, sum xxx$li$. Residue between sons Richard Wenman, W$^m$ Fermor and Rich. Fermer, whom I make executors.

Witnesses: S$^r$ John Whiting, S$^r$ William Poole, Will. Shepard, John Repon, John Welyms, Thomas Streche, and many others (not named).

Proved 26 May 1501, John Reynold proxy for the executors. (Moone, 22.)

ROBERT WYMOND, Citizen and Mercer of London, and Merchant of the Staple of Calais.

### 26 Juyne 1506.

Soul to Almighty God. Bodye in christen sepulture in suche place as shall please God to purvey and ordeyn. Debts to be paid. All goods, etc., to be divided into three portions. 1st, one part to wife Mawde to her propre use, according to the custome of London. The second to my children equally. The third to the use of my will. To High Aulter of St. Albone in Wood Strete xx$^s$. To the two churches in Melborne ij$^s$. To the chapel of St. Nicholas in Kyngs Norton x$^s$. To repair of Swerston brigge x$^s$. To wife in the name of Rewarde xxvi$li$. xiii$^s$ iiii$^d$. To Elizabeth Fenton, my kinswoman and servant, x$li$. To apprentice William Lucy xx$^s$. To William Coke, kynsman and servant, xx$^s$. To kinsman Richard Wymonde, grocer, a rynge of gold. To the werkes of the body of St. Albones in Wode Strete xx$^s$. Prisoners of Ludgate, Newgate, the Counters, Kynges Benche and Marchalseye iij$^s$ iiij$^d$. For a scoler studying divinity v yeres xx marks at the discretion of Doctor Yonge parson in Honey Lane. To my five sisters as many marks. To John Pultrell xx$^s$.

To William Pultrell his servant xx$^s$. If Andrew Fuller take to wife Elizabeth Fenton my cousin he to have xx marks, if not the xx marks passes to my wife. To Steven Jenyns, citizen and alderman of London, v marks. The like to Richard Wymonde, citizen and grocer of London. Overseer Dr. John Yonge v marks. Residue between my five sisters. To Mawde my wife all goods and lands in Derbyshire till my son be 21. My wife with Stevyn Jenyns, Richard Wymonde and Thomas Fuller, executors.

Witnesses: Sir Rogers, parish priest of St. Albans, W$^m$ Carkeke, scrivener, and others. Proved at Lamehithe 29 Oct. 1507. (Adeane, 27.)

RICHARD WYMOND, Citizen and Grocer of London.

23 Aug. 1508.

Soule to God, Our Lady and all the holy company of Hevyn. Body to be buried in the church of S$^t$ Mildred in Brede Strete before the aulter of S. Nicholas and S$^t$ Katherine. To the High Aulter iij$^s$ iiij$^d$. The executors to provide a marble stone with the ymages of me, my wife and children, and a plate over gilt with scripture according. To the garnysshing of the said aulter xl$^s$. Towards a sute of copes x marks. To the high altar of the church of Staumford, co. Lincoln, a torch worth vj$^s$ viij$^d$, and an honest banner for the crosse of the ascention of our Lord with my marke and the grocers armes. To the church of Longburgh, co. Leicester, a banner cloth, the reversion of my tenement there in which Richard Corbett dwelleth. To the church there, to be prayed for, and 10s. for a trental there. To each house of the freres in London vi$^s$ viij$^d$. To Newgate x$^s$, the like to Ludgate, the Counters of London and the Marschalsey. To the high aulter of Seynt Martyn at Ludgate xx$^s$. To the four laser houses next London xi$^d$ each. Repair of the highway at Hakeney xxvi$^s$ viij$^d$. To the church werke at Sheperton xx$^s$ for a dirige and masse of Requiem. To Robert Wolworth all my balances, weights and boxes and xl$^s$. To my maid Agnes a gown of violett, and a kirtell, and vi$^s$ viij$^d$. To Rauffe Alleyne and Rob$^t$ Wolworth a third of my debts in Wallys. To the tenants of my Lord of Burgevenny in Pater noster Row iiij$^d$. To Hakeney Church vi$^s$ viij$^d$. My tenants in the Ryall iij$^s$ iiij$^d$. Sempey Fraterer his debts. To Robert Straker, butcher, xx$^s$. To the parissishioners of S$^t$ Mildred that paid to the kyngs money at the last payement vi$^d$ and under, as moche money as they paid. ij poor women in Hoggen Lane 10$d$. each. To Johanne Blissett iiij$^d$. To the Salters almes folkes in Allhalowen in Bredestrete iiij$^d$. To my kinswoman, a Sadelers wife in Derby, vi$^s$ viii$^d$. I pardon Lord of Burgevenny x$li$. of the xx$li$. he oweth me, and the Dymond to be delivered to him. To Robert Morton all my household stuff that was his moders at Alford in Midd. To John Baxter and Joane his wife my tenement at Byllerica. To Margery my daughter, if she marry with Robert Morton, all my lands in the Ryall. To Elizabeth my daughter my lands in S$^t$ Nicholas Shamells and Hakney, but if Margery do not marry Robert, she to have Elizabeths portion and Elizabeth hers. Johanne my wife to be executrix with Henry Adye and William Campyon. Overseers: Sir Laurence Aylemer, kt., John Yong, parson of Allhalowen in Honey lane. No witnesses.

Proved at Lamehithe, 25 Jan. 1508, by Joane the relict. (Bennet, 10.)

MARGERY WYMOND, maydyn, daughter of Richard Wymond, citizen and Grocer of London.

17 Dec. 1518.

Soul to Almighty God, the Blessed Mary and All Saints. Body in the Collygynall Church of Sent Thomas of Acres in London nyghe the aulter of S$^t$ Thomas in the body of the church. To the High Aulter of S$^t$ Pancras vi$^s$ viii$^d$. At burial a trentall of masses half at S$^t$ Thomas's, half at S$^t$ Mildred's in Brede Strete, where my father lieth, xi$^s$. To Thomas Rawlins, gent., servant to the Lord Cardinall, l mercs out of the c mercs the Maire and Guylde hall of London oweth me. If he aid my executor and brother John Baxster to recover the said c mercs. The other l mercs to priests to syng for my soul. To cosin Agnes Edmonds my furre of grey if Thomas Rawlins will consent. Cosyn Margaret Baxster my gowne furred with shanks. To my sister Johan Baxster my kirtell of tawney worsted and my newe furre of shanks. To Cosyn Margaret Baxster my Beadys of Gold and my dymescent of silver and gilt. To Agnes Wattes a Black dressed goune, ij blacke kirtells, a violett kirtell and ij Ribbends silke. Cosyn Margaret Baxster my gowne of Pewke. To Dorothy Gateley a gowne of blacke. To Mother Agnes my keper iij$^s$ iiij$^d$. To Sir Thomas Kervet my gostely father xiij$^s$ iiij$^d$. To Mr. Stennynges my bedes of Ducketts. To Mr. Cleysey my Reubey set in gold. To my brother John Baxster a ryng of gold. To my sister Johan Baxster my little gennew Ring. Brother John Baxster, executor.

Witnesses: Sir Thomas Kervet, clerk, Robert Thomson, John Adams, William Knight, Richard Lany, Edward Lyckbery. All Lands to Johan, wife of John Baxster, my sister.

Proved at Lamhith 23 Feb. 1518. (Ayloffe, 15.)

Dame ELIZABETH THURSTON of London, widow, late wife of Sir John Thurston, knight, citizen and alderman of London, deceased (formerly wife of Thomas Wymond).

### 21 March 1520.

Soul to God Almighty, our blessed Lady Saint Mary and all the Holy and blessed Company of Hevyn. My body to be buried in the church of S$^t$ Vedast in London in the grave where John Thurston lyeth buried. To the high awter there xx$^s$. To the high awter of S$^t$ Magne beside London brigge xx$^s$. To the high awter of S$^t$ Mary Wolnothe xx$^s$. My Executors to provide against my burying xviii convenient torches and iij great tapers of wax to brenne about my body, and that xxii pour honest men bere and holde the same, each to have xvi$^d$ for his labour, and a gowne of fryse blak or white, and after the said torches to be given to churches: to S$^t$ Vedast iij, S$^t$ Mary Wolnoth ij, S$^t$ Magne ij, S$^t$ Martyn in the Vyntrer ij, S$^t$ Mary Stanynge i, The Chapel of our Lady Berkyng beside the Towre of London ij, chapel of our Lady of Crome ij, the parishe church of Stevenhithe ij. To the high awter at Stevenhithe xx$^s$. To the parishe churche of White Chapell ij torches and to the high altar there vj$^s$ viij$^d$. To every of the fyve orders of Freres in the city of London xiij$^s$ iiij$^d$ to bring my body to its burying place and also iiii$li$. that they may sing trentalls of masses in their churches and pray for my soul, the soul of John Thurston and all cristen soules, and that my executors provide a prest to sing for my soul in

S$^t$ Magne, and for the soule of John Kyrkebye, vynter, late my husband, and for all Xsen soules for the next three yeres, and also to assist at the services there; and the like in the church of S$^t$ Mary Wolnoth to sing for the souls of myself, John Lewes and Thomas Wymonde, and to assist in the services, and I give viii*li*. yerely for his wages. My executors to provide a preest to synge and pray within the church of Strode in Kent, for the soul of Henry Tenacre my graunfather, my fader and moder and all cristen soules, and to receive x marcs yerely. To the same church of Strode, a crosse with Mary and John of silver gilt worth xx*li*., and 3 awter clothes panyd with satyn and velvet figury for iii awters within the said churche, and I wyll that my armes and the armes of the said Sir John Thurston with a picture of the Trinitie embrowdered [be thereon]. To the Companye of Vynterers of London a cuppe with a couer siluer gilt of viii*li*. or the said sum in redye money that they pray for the soule of John Kyrkeby. Towards an exhibition of two Pulpitt men, one at Oxford, the other at Cambridge, 20 marcs sterling, each to have fyve marcs yerely for ij yeres, and that they pray for the soules of Sir John Thurston, late my husband, and the souls of Alice and Alice late his wives. To four maiden's marriages xl*li*. To amend highways about London xx*li*. To the Prior and Convent of Charterhouse xx$^s$. To the Charterhouse at Shene xx$^s$. To the old werke of the cathedral of S$^t$ Paul's vj$^s$ viij$^d$. To the Brotherhede of Jesus founded in the crowd$^l$ of the same churche vj$^s$ viij$^d$. To the Brotherhede of Our Lady and S$^t$ Thomas in the church of S$^t$ Magne xx$^s$. To the Brotherhede of the three score preests in London vj$^s$ viij$^d$. Unto the Brotherhede of Clerks in London to pray for my soule vj$^s$ viij$^d$. To the prison houses of Ludgate, Newgate, the Marshalsye and the Kyngs Bench, vj$^s$ viii$^d$ to be bestowed in brede, and the like in Bethlem. To each of the Lazarhouses for the like vj$^s$ viij$^d$. To poor householders in S$^t$ Vedast, S$^t$ Magne and S$^t$ Mary Wolnoth, 20*li*. That my executors provide a daily masse for the name of Jhū on Friday, a mass of our Lady on Saterday, and daily two Salves, one before the Rood, the other before our Lady, in Priksonge in the church of S$^t$ Vedast and in S$^t$ Magne, and in some other London church for evermore. To the building of the steple of Lye in Kent vj*li*., and xx marcs for a hanging of arrass for Goldsymythes Hall.

To the gilding of the Tabernacle of our Lady in S*t* Vedasts 10*li*., and for the gilding of my awter table to be set upon the awter of our Lady there xx*li*., and a vestment of cloth of gold with the arms of Sir John Thurston and my owne thereupon. To John Caunton, my son-in-law, all my lands in Bednall grene in Stevenhith. To him and Maude his wife, my daughter, 300*li*. To Nicholas their son 100*li*. To Elizabeth Cawnton 100*li*. To Phillip Dollyng, my son-in-law, and Alice his wife 200*li*. To Roger, Johane, Agnes and John, their sons and daughters, xl*li*. each. To Johane Mede my daughter 100*li*., and if she die under age or single, half to Mawde my daughter and half to Alice Dollyng. To Dame Amy my daughter, prioress of S*t* Laurence in Canterbury, xl*li*. To buy lands for their sisterhood xx*li*. To the said Dame Amy a fetherbed, etc., brass and pewter set aside for her in a baskett, also a blak gowne furred with mynks, and a kirtell of chamlett, my bed in the chapel chamber with sparñ of silke, etc. To Mawde my daughter my gowne furred with mynks, my best gurdell and best ringe with a diamond. To my daughter Alice Dollyng my bed with pillars, with celour and testour of chaungeable damaske panyed, and with curteyns of grene sarsnet, etc., my gowne of murrey furred with graye, and a gown of violet furred with shanks, and my best kirtell, a ringe of golde, a pair of beds of golde and girdell of silver with barrys, etc. Unto Johnne Mede my daughter a blak gowne furred with gray, a kirtell of worsted, a gurdell a pendauut, and a pair of beds of corall. To Elizabeth Caunton a gurdell of lowe werke, a pair of beds of silver, a pomander of silver, a gowne of murrey sengle and a kirtell of chamlett, etc., rest of apparel among my said four daughters. Gowne of skarlet lined, to be sold. To John Cawnton a gowne of violett furred with furr orlyaunce. To Phillipp Dollyng a gowne furred with bogye. Unto the wife of my cosyn Daunsey a gurdell of stole werke and a pair of silver beds. To wife of cosyn White a gurdell of silver and a pair of corall beads. To wife of Cosyn Barett a pair of silver beads and a gurdell of stole werke. To Sir Thomas Exmewe, kt., xx*li*. To William his son x*li*. To Elizabeth his daughter x*li*. To Johane Faken the elder xl*s*. To Johane Fakon the younger xl*li*. To her sister xl*s*. The abbot of S*t* Augustine's, Canterbury, a rynge of golde worth iiij*li*. To Dom. Dover monk there v*li*. To Dom.

Holingbourne monk there xl$^s$. To Dom. Xroferson monk there xl$^s$, and to the residue xx$li$. to pray for my soul. To Thomas Typlady, Thomas Yong and Thomas Lamkyn, xx$li$. each to carry out my will and that of Sir John Thurston, with the terms of years of my apprentices and certain Bedding and naperye. To Brings my servant v$li$. to continue in service. Legacies to other servants, viz., William Hoo, Gybons, Richard Crochington, Ryder, Robert Dayken. To apprentices Thomas Michell iiij$li$. To Richard Scott towards his freedom xx$^s$. To Great John xx$^s$. To John Lowth xx$^s$. To chapleyn Sir James x$li$. To Margaret Castell xl$^s$. To Johanne Book xl$^s$. To Anne Kyrwyn xl$^s$. Cosen Rypon of Lye v$li$. Servant Johane Byrd v$li$. Rauf xx$^s$. Lawrence, my servant at Myle ende, xx$^s$. Margaret Childers xx$^s$. Thomas Fryser, who wrote my will, xl$^s$. Richard Kele xl$^s$. Borough and his wife xl$^s$. Gowns to Maister Broke, Justice of Common Pleas, and his wife, Maister Exmewe and his wife, Maister Monox and his wife, Master Munday and his wife, Maister Mylbonne and his wife, Maister Fenrother and his wife, Maister Holderness and his wife, Maister Worley and his wife, Maister Spencer and his wife, Maister Senner and his wife, Maister John Barett and his wife, Maister Vicar of Croydon, Conell and his wife, Richard Corbet and his wife, Mr. Palmer, Baily Mercer and his wife, Richard Masham and his wife, Cosyn Rypon and his wife, William Lowth and his wife, John Broune and his wife, John Twyselton and his wife, John Caunton and his wife, Phillip Dollyng and his wife and children, John Daunsey and his wife, Thomas Barrett, tailour, and his wife, Robert Sayles and his wife, Thomas Foster, Mortymer Browderars, Thomas Gale and his wife, Richard Calard and his wife, William Bully and his wife, John Burton and his wife, my Lady Debenham, Richard Thurston and his wife, John Worshopp and his wife, James Ingleton and his wife, Henry Gery and his wife, Thomas Butler and his wife, my chapleyn, John Laurens, clerk, and his wife, the Sexton of the church, Thomas Fryser and his wife, Elizabeth Brown, Elizabeth Calard, Elizabeth Lamkyn, god-daughters, Frances and Cecile Typlady and all my household servants. To Parnell, preest of S$^t$ Magnus, a gown or xx$^s$. Residue to executors, John Caunton, Mawde his wife, and William Lowth, citizen and goldsmyth. Overseers: Maister Broke, Justice of Common

Pleas, John Brown, payntour, John Dauntsey, mercer, Thomas Barrett, Taillour, Robert White, Draper. To William Lowth my Pyllar bed with celour and testour of grenesaye, etc.

Witnesses: John Pyke, goldsmith, Thomas Gale, Robert Baxster, haberdashers, Sir James Hynde, preest, Thomas Typlady, John Lamkyn, Thomas Fryser and others. Proved at Lamehithe 2 May 1521.

(Maynewaryng, 23.)

### John Wymonde of Rye, co. Sussex.
### 25 July 1529.

Soule to Almightye God, to our Blessed Lady Saint Mary, and to all the Holye Companye of Hevyñ. Body to be buried in the church of Oure Ladye at Rye. To son William oon hundred poundes sterling when 21. To son Richard as much. To dau. Brygett l*li*. at marriage. To dau. Agnes the like. If any die, share to pass to remainder. If all die, to wife Alice. To Moder Joane Weymond x*li*. Brother Robert Wymond vi*li*. xiii$^s$ iiij$^d$, two of my best Gounes, my jaket of velvet and my two horses. To Joane Gyles v*li*. Residue to wyfe. She and brother Robert to be executors. Feoffment made to brother Robert Wymond and John Eston of Rye. To allow wife to hold house in Myddell Streete with remainder to two sonnes, with remainder to daughters, and then to next of blode.

Witnesses: John Coveley, Customer of Chichester, Robert Gaymer, James Byver, John Somer.

Proved 26 Aug. 1529 on oath of John Coveley and Jas. Byver, and Robert Wymonde and Alice the relict, by John Osborne, proxy. (Jenkin, 10.)

### Richard Wenman of Wittney, Oxon.
### 20 Oct. 1533.

Soul to Almightie God, Jhu my redemer and Savio$^r$, and to our blessed Ladye Sainte Mary the Virgin and all the holly companye of hevin. My bodye to be buried in the chapel of the most glorious Resurrection, sett in the pishe churche of Wytney. To the high aulter of the same for tithes and offerings forgotten, and that the curate there will have my soule recomendyd in his devoute praiers, 13s. 4d. To the Cathedral Church of Lincoln 12d. Every stonding light in the church of Wittney, three pounds wex, reddy made, there to berne at the tyme of my exequies and funerall s'vice and other festivall daies as long as they maye thereunto endure. Towardes the reparaccioun of the bells in the Steple 40s. To everyche of five score pore men and women, 6 yardes of cotton of the price of 6d., to make a gowne. To euery of the four orders of Friars in Oxforde; to praie for my soule, the soules of my father and mother, our benefactours souls, and all xten soules, 6li. 13s. 4d.; to be distributed and deliverued unto them in vitayles, w'in the space of five yeares, at Cristmas and Lent, 26s. 8d. To the poore prisoners in the Castel of Oxford, 50s. in Vytayles. To the amendinge of the Highwayes betwyne Milton and Abingdone, 13li. 6s. 8d. The Lease of the Parsonage of Evenly, held of the Prior and Convent of Huntingdon, dated 28 Feb. 4 Hen. 8, to the Vicar and Churchwardens of Wittney, they to distribute therefrom 12li. 8s. 2d. in alms and to keep a solemn obit in their Church with placebo and dirige over night, and a masse of Requiem on the morrow, and to pay 4 almesmen clene of body, aboue the age of threescore yeres, dwelling in the same pish, on Saturday after Evensong, 3s. 4d., viz., tenn pence each, they to be at the parish church every day of the yere between the hours of 7 and 10, and to sing there our Ladys savter or dirige. The Vicar and Churchwardens to pay the Curate 8d., to each priest 4d., to the 2 clerks 4d. To the 4 children 4d., to the bellman 3d., to the bellringer at the mass 4d., for cakes and drynkes 12d., one half penny loffe to the rode light. For 4 tapers of wex to burn about the herse the tyme of my exequies, 20d. For 4 torches at the dirige and mass 16d. For offerings 1d. To 4 poore men holding the same 4 torches, 2d each. To the officyall or comissarye of the Deanry there, to see that the yerely obite be kept, 3s. 4d. The residue of the profits of the parsonage of Evenly to be kept in a chest with two keyes, one to be kept by the churchwardens, the other by the bayliffes of the burgh of Wittney, to be used for the reparacion of the church. To wife Anne 1000 marks in reddye monye, and half of all my household naperye, brasse and pewter, and certain plate; she to occupy the psonage of Coggs and have the profites of Wytney Park, the farm of Holwell, and the cattle there, during life; kepinge hir soole. She to have all lands in Wittney and the borough of Carsewell. To son Thomas 2000 marks, the other half of my goods, and my interest in the farm of Lewe and Senhampton. Elizabeth, wife of my brother William Farmer, a juell of 10 marks. To John Deuereux, notary. A good prist to pray for my soul in the chapel of the Resurrection, 4*li*. yerely. To each poor maid married at Wittney within a year, 25*s*. and 14 lbs. of wool for a garment agaynst their marriage. Repair of highway from Newland to Flemyngefold, 6*li*. 13*s*. 4*d*. Coz. Rich. Humphrey 20*s*. Fabyan his son 40*s*., Thomas Newman 20*s*., and my cosen his wife 20*s*. To Alice Hewins 25*s*., to Joane Cooke 20*s*. and a todde of wool, Turnoure my servant 10*s*. and a todd of wool. On the morrow of my monthes mind a mass be done at Eton College, the provost to be present, 20*d*. And to every skoller being there at scole and residente at my dirige and mass, 2*d*., and to the scole maister being like wise p'sent at the same mass, 3*s*. 4*d*. And I will that after dinner on the same day the scolers there may have a recreation to sporte them, and they shall saie for my soule and all cristen soules the psambe *de profoundis*. Residue to son Thomas, he to be executor. Brothers William and Richard Farmer coadjutors, Thomas Gifford, Esq., overseer. To Mary w. of Tho. Gifford a juell worth 5 marks. Ursula my daughter, Thomas Wenman's wife, for a juel 5*li*. To her son Richard my godson, 10*li*., and to his brothers Harry, William, and Thomas 10*li*., and to Anne and Elizabeth Wenman 100 marks. Thomas Wenman my cosin 10*li*.

Proved at Lamehithe 18 Dec. 1534 by Thos. Dacuraye, notary, proxy for Thomas. (Hogen, 21.)

### Anne Wenman of Wyttney.
#### 22 Nov. 1535.

Hole of mynde and in my good memory being, lawde be it unto Almighty God .... my soule unto God Almighty, Jesu my Redem[r] and Saviou[r] and to our blessed Lady Saint Mary the Virgin, his most glorious mother, and to all the holy company of hevyn .... my body to be buried within the parishe churche of our blessed Lady of Wyttney w'in the Tombe nyghe Richard Wenman late my husband. I bequeth unto the high awter xij$^d$, to the cathedrall churche of Lincoln iiij$^d$. I will that there be a tapre of twoo poundes of wax kept before the Trinitie, by the space of one yere aftre my deceas, and to every standing light in the same church a tapre of twoo pounds of wax. Item to the bells x$^s$. Item to the torche light for brennyng at my Exequies, my moneth mynde, and my yeres mynde, x$^s$. Unto Thomas Mydwynter my brother xx$^s$ st. To Elizabeth my sister xx$^s$ yerely during her lyfe. My scarlet gowne unto maistres Ursula my daughter-in-lawe, if she will were it, yf not I geve it unto maistres Doweley. Item I geve my sattyn kirtell unto Maistress Ursula. I geve to William, sonne of the forsaid Thomas Mydwynter, xli. To Sir Peter Raynolds, my cosyn and godson, xl$^s$. To Richard Reynolds xxvj$^s$ viij$^d$, and to Alice his suster xx$^s$, and to her children twoo todds of wolle. Item to Anne Dyer my god-daughter xx$^s$ and one todde of wolle. To Frauncis Higgs my god sonne xiij$^s$ iiij$^d$. To Robert Lowe my godsonne l$^s$. To every other god-childe iiij$^d$. To Richard, William, Thomas, Henry, Gifford, Anne and Elizabeth, children of Thomas Wenman, my sonne, xli. each. To Henry Wenman all my shepe at Taynton or elsewhere; if he die before 21, to be parted among his brethren and sisters. To Master Ellys Warham, vicar of Wyttney, xiij$^s$ iiij$^d$. To John Terrolde xiij$^s$ iiij$^d$. To Richard Chemson, xiij$^s$ iiij$^d$. John Richards xiij$^s$ iiij$^d$. To Giles Bromfelde my servant xl$^s$. To John Rede xiij$^s$ iiij$^d$. To Rob$^t$ Dunverde v$^s$. To Joane Cooke my servaunt vj$^s$ viij$^d$. To Elizabeth Storkey my servaunt xiij$^s$ iiij$^d$. I geve my gurdell w'th blak frynged sides and golde in the myddell unto goodwife Yette. My murrey gowne furryd w'th Calabre unto the good wyfe Dyer, my murrey gowne, purfelde w'th velvet, unto the goodwyfe Tempull, my blak gowne purfeld with velvet unto the good wife Gerey, but I will that the velvet be taken of before the gowne deliuered. My silke chamlet kyrtell unto the good wife Webbe. I geve my blak gowne purfeld w$^t$ tawneye velvet unto the forsaid Joane Coke my servaunt, my twoo blak worsted kirtells unto Elizabeth Storkey and Agnes Byddell my servaunts. Residue to Thomas my son, the Executor.

Witnesses: Leonard Yate, Sir John Richards, Andrew Sayley, Richard Secoll and Sir Roger Clempson.

Proved 20 March 1537 by Thomas Docwra, proxy for Thomas the son. (Drugile, 15.)

### John Wayman of Suffolk.

### 14 Julye 1543.

John Wayman in the countie of Suff. in the diocese of Norwyche, maryner, being of good mynde and memorye, thankes geuen to oure Lord Jhu Criste, made this his will nu'cupative, by the whiche he gave all his goodes movable and vnmovable, debts, redy monney and apparell.... unto John Fraunces of Ippiswiche, vtherwyse called maryner, whom he made and ordeynd to be his executour .... at what tyme was present Robart Martyn, Thomas Wright and Robart Benson.

Probate 1 April 1546 on the oath of John Thorpe. (Alen, 6.)

### William Wymonde of Rye, co. Sussex.

### 1 Edw. 6 (1547).

Soule to God Almightie. Body to be buryed in the Church of Rye, beside my father, John Wymonde. To be bestowed uppon the high waies betwene Tonbrige and Rye, £10. To the setting up of the Almes House in Rye, £5. To Palle Wymonde, £100. Also to Joane Wymonde, my dau., £40. To my son Frauncis, 20 crownes, and my best cape and jacket of clothe. To my godson Will'm Pedred, £5. To Colett my woman, £3. To Peter de Hergat, £3. The rest being by estimacion £400 I give my 3 sonnes in equal portions shifted between them. To John Wymonde my son, all my land and ten'ts in Icklesham, Gestling, and Facarlye, and my house called "Grene Halle" in Rye, with my shoppes at Strand. To Wittm my sonne, all my lands in Stone, and Witnesham, and my house in Myddell Streate in Rye, to be faire built with my brick now at my cosin John Elton's flote. To Palle Wymonde my sonne, my lands in Ivecherche, and my principall tenement in Rye, with all my lande and housing lying adjoyning unto the same. Cosen John Eston to be Executour, to se my children brought up to Scole. I give him £20 by yere out of my lands till my said children com to lawfull age. Nothing made of wallnut tree to be taken from my principall tenement, but all to remayne to my sonne Paule. If John Eston dye, M$^r$ John Binckens of London to be executour, if he dye John Stocks of London. If my sons die my dau. to inherit, if she die £500 to the highwayes, and rest between the children of Robert Wymound, my Uncle, and John Eston's sons.

Witnesses: Edmund Stambler, Vicar of Rye, Thomas Birchett, John Davyson, John Best, and Will. Greneflat.

Proved 15 March 1551 on oath of John Eston. (Powell, 8.)

HENRY WAYNEMAN, clarke.
16 Oct. 1556.

Soule unto Almightie God my maker, redemer and onlye Saviour. Bodie to be buried within the churche of S$^t$ Buttolphe within Aldersgate, in suche convenient place of the churche as shalbe thought meete by myn' executors. The fourtie shillings whiche I owe unto my frende Jasper Palmer, as also all my debts, to be well and trulye paide. To my brother Nicholas Wayneman £13 10s. 0d., cum'yng and growinge upon my benefice of Donnyngton for half a yeres rent. I geve to him the £10 owinge me by Thomas Tyrrell. To John Hochinson, sadler, 10s. out of the 25s. he dothe owe me. I wyll Anne Tyrrell shall have delyvered to her all suche thinges as remayned in my handes at the making hereof, bequethed and given unto her by Elyn Tailor, granmother unto the said Anne, that is to say, one salte with cover parcell gilte, fyue spones with mayden heads, a diaper table clothe, a playne table clothe, a diaper towell, a playne towell, a dozen of newe napkyns, sixe diaper napkyns, two payer of sheets, a chafing dish and certeyn pewter. I give my brother Nicholas 20s. owinge unto me by John Cogham, scrivener, and the rest of my goods and cattals, he to be executour.

Witnesses: Robert Harrison, curate of the parish, Jasper Palmer.

Probate 7 Nov. 1556 by Nicholas. (Kechyn, 21.)

## WAYMAN WILLS.

RYCHARD WAYMAN of Hydnam, Beds.

3 Sept. 1558.

Sycke in bodye and hole in mynde. Soule unto Almightye God my only Sauyour and Redemer, to take me to his greate mercye. Bodye to be buryed in crysten buryall, wheare it shall chaunce me to departe this worlde. I giue and bequethe unto my sonne Rychard Wayman, after the decesse of my mother and me, all suche landes and possessyons as apperteynythe to my mother and me, and hys heyrs of hys bodye . . . . and for lacke of yssue . . . . to Rychard my brother, Wyllyam Wayman's sonne, and for lacke of yssue . . . . to my daughter Elizabethe, and so forthe to my next heyres for euer. Unto Rychard my sonne, £40 a thadge of one and Twentye yeres, and yf that yt plesethe God to call hym to hys mercye before y$^t$ he comethe to the adge aforesaid, . . . . unto my daughter Elizabeth. To the said Elizabeth £40. To my mother Elizabethe Tayller £20. Unto my syster Ales Haren, wydowe, £10, and to euery one of her chyldren . . . . 40s. . . . . at the adge of 18. Unto my brother Willyam Wayman's chyldren, Rycharde and Elizabeth, 5 markes eche at the adge of 18. Whereas Xrofer Wylshyr dothe owe me Four poundes tenne shillinges . . . . I clerelye forgyue it hym. I do make Margarett my wyff my full exectryx, and Robart Tayler of Steventon my other executor . . . . and bequethe unto hym fyve markes, and to my wyfe the reste of my goodes. I make Rychard Larrens of Bedford the Supervysor and overseer of this my will and given him seven nobells for his paynes.

Witnesses: Henry Atkytson, Vycar of S$^t$ Pulkers in London, John Denham, Rob$^t$ Shawe, citizen and alle brewer of London, Xrofer Wyllshyr, Rychard blackwell.

Probate 21 Sept. 1558 on oath of Edmund Brudenell, proxy for Margarett. (Noodes, 46.)

WILLIAM WENMAN of Fringford, co. Oxon, gent.

2 June, 28th Elizabeth (1586).

Body to be buried in the chancel at Fringford. To daughter Ellen alias Eleanor an annuity of £20 to be paid half yearly in the church of Fringford, she to marry any good and honest man that will assure her in land £20 a year. I also bequeath her £200 to be paid in the church porch of Fringford. To daughter Elizabeth £80. To sons Frauncis and Giles £10 each, and two annuities of 10s. each. To Alice Garratt 5s. My executor to bestow on Elizabeth Busbye and Thomas Rowe "as by Godes providence they weare lefte to me." To son Fraunces a further £10 out of sums due to my deceased wife. The like to son Giles, daughter Elizabeth, daughter Fraunces, daughter of son Fraunces £10. My soule I give to Jesus Christ. Residue to Richard Wenman, my son and heir, my sole executor.

Witnesses: William Wenman, Junior, Fraunces Wenman, Giles Wenman, Robert Dimock and John Bunne.

Proved at London 8 Nov. 1588. (Leicester, 5.)

WILLIAM WYMAN of Buxsted, co. Sussex, yeoman.

15 July 1589.

Soul to Almighty God. Bodye to be buried in the church of Buxsted. To my wife Margaret an annuity of £10 out of the lands of Robert Wells, gent., but if Robert repay the £100 he oweth, the annuity to cease. I also give her a bond of £22, by which William and Roger Dopp stand bound to me, and also another for the like sum which John Benguyn and William Awcock owe me, and another of £11 which the said Awcock and Thomas Sleache owe, and another of the like which Thomas Martyn and John James owe, and yet another of the like due from Thomas Baylye and Alexander Owsborne of Goodherst, and another of £11 due from Henry Bambrooke, vicar, and Thomas Awcocke of Marke street, and another of the like in which Robert Hoode and Henry Hoode of Maresfield stand bound, and another of the like in which Richard Burgess and Thomas Hooke stand bound. To John Bulton, my wife's son, £20. To Agnes, daughter of the said John, £10, and to the child his wife now goeth with £10, and if the said child die it shall go to Joane the mother. To Robert Wyman, my unkind brother, £5. To Thomas Baylye 20s. To John Kenwarde's wife 20s. To Walter Quay, Susanna Payne and Margaret Venell, my servants, 6s. 8d. each. To Barbary, wife of John Ades, 6s. 8d. To Margaret Hoyge 20s.

Residue to my wife Margaret, she to be executrix, and Edmonde Woode of Uckfield my overseer.
Witnesses: William Cadman and John Ades.
Proved 5 Aug. 1589 by Anthony Lawe, notary public, proxy of Margaret. (Leicester, 66.)

ELIZABETH, dau. of Sir RICHARD WENMAN, Knight, and Dame ISABELL his wife.
7 Dec., 33 Eliz. (1590).

Soul to Thalmighty God. Body to the earthe from whence it came. Executor, my well beloved Roger Hackett. Lord and Lady Norreys, the sum of £50 to be made into pieces of plate in remembrance of my goodwill. To Sir John and Sir Henry Norreys £20 to be made into twoe rings for them. My sister Margery £100. Brother Frances Wenman £100. George Calfield, Esq., £50. Cosen Maximillian Norreys, Esq., £100. Phillip Cubbidge, my maid servant, £25. Sibbile Huddlestone, widow, £10. Godson Richard Purfrey £5, his sister Elizabeth Purfrey £5. To M$^{rs}$ Dannett and M$^{rs}$ Cotten 20s. each for rings. Two maides of the house that watch with me 20s. To the poor £5. To Rich$^d$ and Tho. Wenman, my eldest brother, £5 for a ring. The better part of apparell to sister Margery, but the worsest sorte to Phillip Cubbidge. The newe gowne she is making to Mrs. Cotten. Residue to Executor.
Witnesses: John Broughton, Richard Hountes his mark, Thomas Brookes his mark.
Commission granted to Frauncis Wenman, brother of deceased, to administer 29 Jan. 1590-1. (Sainherbe, 1.)

JOHN WYMOND of Lanhidrocke.
10 April, 33 Eliz. (1591).

Soule unto Almightie God my creator, and to Jesus Christe his sonne, etc., etc. My bodie to xrian buriall in the parish church of Lanridocke. To my sonne Thomas all messuages, lands and tenements in Treffrye, held of John Treffrie, Esq. Also the messuages called Forde or Forthe, held of John Laghar als. Langharne, to a term. To my dau. Lowdye Wymound £40 when 21 or married, so that she marrye with the consent of my son Tho⁵, W^m Glynne, Rich. Courtney, gent., and Constance Hawkinge, her sister, or twoe of them.

No witnesses.

Proved at London 10 Feb. 1591-2 by Fra⁵ Clerke, notary, proxy for Thomas. (Harrington, 16.)

JOHN WYMAN, Yeoman, of East Smithfield in St. Botulphe without Aldgate.

4 Sept. 1593.

Sowle to Almighty God. Body to be buried in decent sorte as executor think meete. Debts to be paid. To father Richard Wyman of East Smithfield £10. To my son Theophilus £50 when 21. To my daughter Phœbe £50 when 21. If son die his part to pass to daughter and contrariwise. Residue to wife Elizabeth. Bernard Carter, notary publique and citizen, and Humfrey Rowland of East Smithfield, horne breaker, to assist my wife as executrix.

Witnesses: Humphrey Rowland, Edward Shorter, William Laiman, Edmund Cordwell, John Hill, John Baker, servant to Bernard Carter.

Proved at London 26 Sept. 1593 by Thomas Warde, notarye public, proxy of Elizabeth. (Nevill, 66.)

RICHARDE WENMAN of Oxforde, gent.

6 April, 40 Eliz. (1598).

Sowle unto God my creator and redeemer. Body to be buryed at the discretion of myne Executors. To Dorothy my welbeloved wief, the manner of Gamadge Hale and all messuadges, etc., in the Co. of Glouc. for terme of her life, but it is not my meaninge that my wiffe shall claime the manner of Gamedge Hale duringe the life of my mother. All my goods to my wife, whome I doe make my sole Executor, prayinge her to buy or provide some Ringes or other pretie Jueles, and to bestowe upon my mother, my brother Lyllie and sister Lyllie, my father and mother Pudsey, my brother Thomas, and to everie one of them. I give my daughter Jane £100 ... to be ymployed and layde out for her best advancement and proffit in bringinge her upp. Wife to enter into a bond to pay when she is 18. If she do not agree da. Jane to be executrix.

Witnesses: Edm. Lillie, Thomas Fytzherbert, Eustace Moore.

Proved 11 May 1598. (Lewyn, 40.)

**JEROMYE WAYMAN** of St. Margaret, Westminster, Gardiner.

10 Nov. 1611.

Soule into handes of Almightie God my creator, and to Jesus Christ his son, etc. Bodie to be buryed in S<sup>t</sup> Margaretts churchyard. To wife Anne all household stuffe and furniture (except one great cupboard with presses), also 4 kyne, 2 stocks of bees standinge at Knightsbridge in the ground I hold of M<sup>r</sup> Glassington. To Bartholemewe Wayman my son, nowe an infant, £70. when 21. If he die to be divided amongst children of Wm. Harrys, my brother-in-law, dwelling at Cublington, Bucks. To the said Barth<sup>w</sup> the great "Cubbord" named above. To Wm. Harrys, his wife and children, £4. To my mother and sister a paire of skye colored garters to make each of them a girdle. To John Brickell in consideration of the 20s. I owe him, given him by my brother John, the lease of land and trees thereon held of M<sup>r</sup> Glassington at Knightsbridge, 1 suit of app'ell, a p' of sparke of velvet hose, a satten dublett, a silke tobine jerkin w<sup>th</sup>out sleves, w<sup>th</sup> a hat lyned with velvet. Unto my Cosen Edward Dudley, my Exec., my sword and dagger with a silver Handell. To Derham my Bugg gowne. For my buriall 50s., and 10 dozen of bread to the poor. Residue to Edw. Dudley.

Witnesses: John Droke, John Marsh, George Miller, Stephen Langdale, servant to Rob<sup>t</sup> Ayraye, Sc.

Proved at London 4 Feb. 1611-12 by Edward Dudly. (Fenner, 15.)

Sentence *re* Nullity of Will of **ANDREW WAYMONT**.

Examined by Sir John Benet, Kt., LL.D., Custos. Re will of Andrew Waymont of S<sup>t</sup> Olave, Southwarke, in cause

inter Margt Miller alias Waymont and Martha Waymont, relict of above. Judgment that the will be nuncupative 9 Aug. 1611.
Read 2 Dec. 1611. (Wood, 105.)

JOHN WYMAN of Newent, co. Glouc., Yeoman.
20 Sept. 1615.

Soul to Almightie God, etc., bodie to the earth. Repar'con of church of Newent iij$^s$ iiij$^d$, and the Markett House there iij$^s$ iiij$^d$, Poor there xl$^s$. To Rich. Dobyns of Newent, gent., and Tho$^s$ George of the same place, clothier, my messuage in which I live, and my other messuage in Newstreete, in the occupacon of Anne Hodges, widow, in trust. The former for the use of Joane my wife for life, if she keep sole, and after to Lawrett my daughter and her coheires and assigns. The other messuage to the use of Joane my wif for 9 years and after a moiety, viz., the Halle and kitchin, lofts and sollers over the same, and part of the garden to John, eldest son of my late brother Thomas Wyman, for life, with remainder to William Wyman the younger, his brother, remainder to Lawrett my daughter. The rest of the house to the use of W$^m$ Wyman the elder, another son of the said Thomas, for life; with remainder to Rich$^d$ his brother; remainder to Lawrett my dau. And yet another part to George son of Thomas Wyman, with remainder to the said Lawrett. The 23$s$. John Fortey oweth. To Rich$^d$ and Anne, two children of my brother-in-law Rich. Arters. To dau. Lawrett 100$li$., the two second best feathebedes, etc., my biggest brasse potte, etc., and six best pewter platters. Johane my wife to be sole executrix. Overseers, Grymbald Pauncefote, gent., Rich. Dobyns, and Tho. George.

Witnesses: Rich. Angworth, Francis Puckmore, W$^m$ Coming, and James Morse.

Proved at London 15 Nov. 1615 by Joane. (Rudd, 111.)

MARTHA WAYMANTE of St. Olave's, Southwarke, widow.
25 April 1618.

Soule to God my Creator, etc. Body to the earth. Son Robert Wilson, cit. and Letherseller of London, all freehold lands and tenements. Dau. Martha, w. of Robert Swanne, £10 and a payer of my fynest shetes. Dau. Joane, wif of Edward Dabber, tenements in Shoreditch and all my wearing apparell, both lynen and woollen, 2 payer of shetes, 2 dozen of diaper napkins and 2 tablecloathes of the coarser sought. Children of Edward Browne, which he had by Mary my eldest dau., £60, viz., to Edward, Thomas, James, Mary, Suzan and Sarah, £10 each. To cozen Cath. Amon 40s. Kinswoman dwelling in Stepney churchyard my Carsey gowne imbroydered with velvett and with buttons on the sleves. Goddau. Martha Powell 40s. Residue to Robert Wilson, the executor.

Witnesses: Wm. Symonds, Thomas, son of Thomas Abbott, &c.

Proved at London 27 Oct. 1618 by Robert Wilson. (Meade, 98.)

PAULE WYMOND the Elder of Whinchilsea, gent.
26 June 1619.

Soul to Almightie God, etc. Poore of Whinchilsea 10s. Dau. Eliz., wif of Jeremye Talhurst, 5s., and Amye, wife of Thomas Pelham, 5s., to be paid within a month of my death. Son William my lattin bookes except a Concordance and my Cooper's Dictionary. Son Paule all household stuffe, with the 2 houses in Rye and my best gown. To John, s. of Tho. Dyne of Lydd, 5s. Sybilla Wymond, my dau., £30. Bridgett Wymond, my dau., £30. Dau. Anne Wymond. Executors, wife Eliz$^{th}$ and son George. Wife 6 silver spoons, my wheate, malte, butter, cheese, poultrie, 4 loads of loggs and 3 loades of faggotts. Residue to George Wymond and all my messuage and land in Stone, I. of Oxney.

Witnesses: John Botting, John Standen, Humphry Hunt.

Proved in London 20 Aug. 1619 by George, the son. (Parker, 81.)

ROBERT WYMAN of Brookethorpe, co. Gloucester, Yeoman.
4 April, 20 Jas. I. (1623).

Soul unto hands of Allmighty God. Body in churchyarde. Poor of Brookethropp 20s. Poor of Harscombe in Harffeylde 40s. Martha and Anne Hole, dau$^s$ of my dau. Julyan Hole, £10 each. Rebecca and Marg$^t$ their sisters £5 each when 21. Hester, dau. of my dau. Alice Miller, £5 when 21. Residue to wife Amye, she to be executrix. Overseers: Rich$^d$ Harrys of Brookethroppe, Thomas Roberts and my son John Wyman.

Witnesses: Poyntz Rolles, Thomas Organ, Rob$^t$ Wathews.

Proved 12 July 1625 by Anne the relict. (Clarke, 79.)

HENRY WENMAN of London, Haberdasher.

Soule to God. Body to the ground. Executor, my brother M$^r$ Thomas Wenman of Soulderne, co. Oxon, to whom I give a gould seale ringe. To brother Richard Wenman of Norwich a wrought capp. To Cosen Edward Thorpe a payre of gloves. To the poor of S$^t$ Faithes, where I live, 40s. Residue to my wife [not named] and son Richard, to be divided between them. Executor, Brother Thomas.

Witnesses: Richard Wenman, Edward Thorpe.

Proved at London 11 May 1632 by Thomas Wenman, brother of deceased. (Audley, 50.)

RICHARD WAYMAN of Birmingham, Ironmonger.

23 July 1633.

Soul unto the Lord God of Heaven, whoe elected mee before the world began, trusting and assuredly beleeeving that by the Death and bountyfull blood sheding of his deare sonne, my onely Saviour and Redeemer Jhesus Christ, after my mortall Life is dissolved, and my filthy body then mortally diseased, that my soule shall p$^r$sently enter into the Celestiall Joyes, there to lyve and continue with all the holy Saynts and Angells. To eldest son Jhosea 20s. Other son Jeremias 20s. If Sarah my wife be with child I doe hereby give and bequeath to the said child 20s. Debts and funeral expenses to be paid. Wife to have residue, and because I knowe it will be great trouble and vexation for my said wife to gather in all my debts, because many of them are casual, and hardly to be begotten, I have appointed Richard Carrles of Birmingham, Yeoman, and W$^m$ Seeley of the same, woollen draper,

Executors, and given each 10s. Overseers : W^m Baker of Birmingham, Ironmonger, and Rob^t Walker of same, glover.

T. : W^m Dickens, W^m Baker, Rich. Pemberton, Scriv^r, and others.

Commission to W^m Glasbrooke, one of the creditors, to administer 11 Nov. 1633. (Russell, 103.)

### Hugh Wayman of Poole, co. Dorsett (nuncupative).
### No date (1635).

Son Robert Wayeman £20. His sister Webster 40s. Residue to wife Dorothy, sole Exec^x.

T. : Suzanna Bramble and his sister Joane Webster.

Proved 28 May 1635 by Dorothy. (Sadler, 54.)

### John Wyman of Barton Street, Glouc.
### 26 Sept., 14 Car. I. (1639).

Soule an Spirrit into the hands of God my Creator, etc. Messuage in Gloucester between the North gates and the west side of the street, in occupation of Rob^t Portman, whose it was, and which I bought of Tho. Hackett, gent. I devise the profits thereof to Margarett my wife, and on her death to the Mayor and Burgesses, for the mending of the Highway from the farm house of Abbots Barton in Barton St. to the Bridge near Scut bridge called Mary bridge. To W^m, son of W^m Mathewes of Barton Street, £50 when 21, but if he die, to the said Mayor and Burgesses for the use of the Bayliff of S^t James' Hospital. The poor of S^t Mary de Lead, whereof I am a parishioner, £5. To Rich. Crowe, my wife's brother, £5, and each of his children, except Richard, 20s., and to the said Rich^d £5. To W^m Wyman, my kinsman, £20, and his children 20s. each, except Francis, who is to receive £10. Marg^t, dau. of W^m Mathewes, dec^d, £5 when 21. Alice Weavour, my wife's sister, 40s., and to James her husband 20s. for a ring. All godchildren 2s. 6d. each. All servants 20s. each. M^r John Halford, preacher, 20s. for a ring. W^m Harris of Hemsteed, Abell Wantner, Steph. Halford, rings. Tho^s Woodcocke my neighbour 10s., James Hosier my neighbour 10s., and 20s. for the use of

Eliz., dau. of Tho. Trowe. To all the children of Jas. Swallowe 10s. each. My wife's kinsman, Rich. Trowe of London, painter, 20s., and to each of his children 10s. Residue to wife Marg$^t$.

T.: Hy. Beard, Steph. Halford, Eliza Halford, Hugh Halford.

Proved 12 Dec. 1640 by Margaret the relict. (Coventry, 27.)

Sir FRAUNCIS WENMAN of Carswell, co. Oxon, Knight.

30 March 1640.

Soul to God. Body in next parish where I die. To eldest son Samuel all my books and papers in my studdy in the house at Carswell. To my wife Lady Anne a messuage in Low, co. Oxon, in the tenure of Simon Yate, and all lands, etc., in Liewe Coggs and Witney, of which I levied a fine 14 Car. I. between me and Sir Henry Raynsford, Kt., until my son and heir be 21, to the use of the Wardship of my son and the maintenance of my daughters and younger children. To younger son Frauncis an annuity of £60. To daughter Ann Wenman £1500, but if she marry without her mother's consent she is to have £500 only, and the other £1000 to be divided between her two brothers. Servants Sarah and Elizabeth Warwicke £3. Servant Leonard Foord a house in Witney for the life of himself and Jane his wife at £4 yearly rent. To servant William Oley a house in Wytney in occupation of John Watkins, paying 40s. rent. Desires the protection of the Countess of Carlisle and the Earl of Holland for his son Samuel. Executrix, Lady Anne my wife. Overseers, Viscount Faulkland and Sir John Danvers of Chellsey, Kt.

Proved at London 16 Feb. 1640 by Lady Anne Wenman the relict. (Leicester, 5.)

THOMAS WAINEMAN of Embsay, co. York, in parish of Skipton, yeoman.

19 Dec. 1655.

Soule into the hands of Almightie God, etc. Bodie to be buryed at the discretion of my freindes. Debts to be paid. Elizabeth my onelie dau. all my goods, chattells, houses and buildings in Embsay when 21; if she die, to pass to William Waineman, my brother-in-law. W^m, John and George Waineman, my Unckles sons, to have £10 each, and Rebeckah Waineman £10. To Sibell Masonn £14. To my brother Christopher Waineman £10. Brother-in-law W^m Wayneman, Executor.

Proved at London 21 May 1656. (Berkeley, 186.)

ROBERT WEYMAN of Cottesham, co. Cambridge, Yeoman.
### 16 Sept. 1655.

Soul into the hands of Allmighty God. Body to be buried in the churchyard. Son John Weyman my black maer colt. Wife Alice one coombe of mesolin, towards her maintenance, and 2 blacke cowes, with the Lodge at the Mill house for her life. Father-in-law John Boram executor, to see my debts paid and body decently brought to earth. To dau. Mary Weyman the little hutch standinge at the beds feete in chamber wherein I lye, with all the lynnen in it, and if any money remains after debts, etc., paid, she is to have it, but all goods are to be sold, and the monies thereof raysed to be imployed to the puttinge out of the two boyes Vincent and Mathew. Alice my wife to have her dwellinge in the great house wherein she nowe lieth, until the 25th of March next, and that the little cottage be repaired.

Witnesses: John Barnes, Edward Haddon, Ralph Haddon, Rob. Mathew, Joseph Mynott.

Proved in London 27 Oct. 1655 by John Boram. (Aylett, 390.)

There is another copy on fol. 392, in which he is styled Robert Waineman.

MARGARETT WAYNEMAN of St. Andrew, Holborne, wid.
### 12 Jan. 1656.

Soule into hands of Almightie God. Bodie to be decentlie buried. Son W^m Wayneman £10 for mourning. 3 dau^s of my sister Ann Hawkes, viz., Anne, Joane, Mary, £20 each, as soon as executors recover sum of £350 from John Dakeine of Furnifalls Inne, gent. Residue, money, plate, jewels, debts, etc., to friends Alkington Painter of Gillingham, Esq., and George Carter of S$^t$ Dunstans in the West, grocer.

Witnesses: Edwd. Brent, Dorothy Baynan, Peter Miles, James Joyner.

Proved in London 20 April 1657. (Ruthen, 119.)

THOMAS WEAMAN of Fillongley, co. War., yeoman.

7 May 1657.

Soule to God that gave it me. Bodie to the earth from whence it came. Eldest son John, The litle house and croft bought of W$^m$ Leightborne, and the Close bought of Henrie Hardinge, lying in Hollyberrie in Merryden. To dau. Elizabeth four score poundes. To son Henry three score poundes. Son-in-law Richard Clark's children, Rich$^d$, Tho$^s$, Isabell and Elzabeth, £7 10s. each when 21. Eliz. Cammell, my grandchild, £5 when 21. The rest of my younger children, Marie, Eleanor, William, Gregorie, Richard and Anne, threescore poundes a peece when 21, but if my son W$^m$ enter into half my purchased lands in Allisley, he shall pay Anne his mother £30 out of the said £60. Eliz. Balle, my sister, 40s. a year. Wife Anne and eldest son John, Exec$^{rs}$. Overseers, Tho$^s$ Cammell and my son Henry.

Witnesses: W$^m$ Stanhurst, Oliver Wheigham, W$^m$ Wheigham.

Proved at London 13 Aug. 1657 by Ann and John. (Ruthen, 301.)

SIR THOMAS WENMAN, Knight, Lord Viscount WENMAN of Tuam in Ireland.

3 Dec. 1658.

Soul to God. Bodie to be interred at Twyford without any manner of pompe. Son-in-law Francis Wenman, Esq., and Vincent Barry of Thame, co. Oxon, to hold all my manors and lands in Oxfordshire for 21 years. To pay my brother Phillip Wenman £1000 yearly, and to give him £1000 within a year of my death to pay his debts. To my daughter Samuell £3000, my daughter Cave £3000. To my grandchild Elizabeth, daughter of my daughter Mary Wenman by Francis her husband, £1000. To my grandson Grevill Verney, Esq., £200. To my two sisters Lady Penelope Dynham and Mrs Jane Martyn £100 each for mourning. Servant John Brooke £120 and a house and land in Twyford in the tenure of John Bevin for 21 years at a rental of 20s. To servant Simon Eaton £5. Land in Wales bought of cousin Morgan and his wife to my grandchild Richard Wenman, with remainder to grandchild Ferdinand Wenman, failing heirs Philip's annuity to pass to Ferdinand at his death, and if he die without issue to Richard his brother, remainder to testator's right heirs. The marriage settlement made for my deceased son Richard, though he died without issue, his interest therein is to pass to son Francis. Lease of the Parsonage of Twyford and lands in Sydnam to go with my manors in Twyford, Charndon, Poundon, and Sydnam, till Ferdinand or his brother come of age. If my debts cannot otherwise be met, the manor of Cobcott and lands there and in Aston-Rowant and Lewknor may be sold. Executors, Francis Wenman and Vincent Barry.

Published 5 Jan. 1664 before Richard Lydall and Tho. King.

*Codicil.*—To Thomas Loveday my servant the house he lives in at a rent of 20s. Mr Canner my chaplain £10. Servant Richard Harper the younger £10. John Tredway, the boy that is under the cook, £5. Thomas Hughes, my fatboy, £5. Mrs Wakefield, my sons Winmans servant, £10. All other servants two years' wages. My hound to my kinsman Thomas May. My family to be kept together 6 months after my death, to give my servants opportunity to find employment. They are to have mourning at my charge. Poor of Twyford £20, of Sydnam £10, of Moreton in Thame £5. Poor of Thame £10.

Signed 6 Jan. 1664.
Witnesses: Thomas King, Thomas Smith.
Proved 6 Feb. 1664 by Francis Wenman. (Hyde, 22.)

WILLIAM WAYNMAN, St. Buttolphes, Sussex, husbandman.

Soul to God my Creator. Body to be buried according to will of my executrix. Children of my sister Margt Goffe £20 when full age. To Uncle Slutter's children, viz., to Anne Slutter £10 when 18 or married, to Mary Slutter, Joane Slutter, and Hester Slutter £10 each on like condition. My sister Alice Rogers £10. To a minister for a funeral sermon 10s. Cousin Anne, wife of Peter Goffe, 20s. To Sarah Munn of Buttolph's 10s. To Nicholas Rich or his wife, widow Orton, and John Belchamber, 10s. to be divided among them. Executrix, my loveing Aunt Mercy Slutter of Buttolphes, widow, whom I trust to for my decent burial, I give her all my land in Ailseford and the rest of my goods.

Proved 26 Aug. 1661 by said Mercy Slutter. (May, 131.)

ROBERT WENMAN of Norwich, mercer.

11 Sept. 1679.

Soul to God, Body to Executrices to be interred. To da. Anne the £300 Son-in-law Nicholas Cock hath covenanted to pay her within 3 months of her marriage. To daughter Anne annuity of £12 out of houses in S$^t$ Peter Mancroft, settled on me after my father and mother's decease, by Robert Hornsey, Alderman of Norwich, my grandfather, 12 Jan. 1633. Houses in White Lyon Street to wife Anne. If Nicholas Cock perform his marriage articles to clear what is due to me as Executor of my father Wenman, then I bequeath to Elizabeth Cock my daughter and Anne Cock my grandchild, a moiety of the said houses, and my daughter Anne the other moiety. Poor of S$^t$ Peter's 20s., Residue to wife Anne and Anne my daughter. Overseers, Francis Bacon, Thomas Bacon and Augustine Briggs, Esq., and my kinsman Richard Wenman, Senior.

Witnesses: Elizabeth Fittes, John Fitz, James Jerkes.

Proved in London 29 Jan. 1684 by Anne the daughter. (Cann, 14.)

SIR FRANCIS WENMAN, Knight and Baronett, of Caswall, co. Oxon.

23 July 1680.

Soul to God, Body at discretion of executor. To my daughter Dorothy £1000 upon a mortgage of lands in

Holywell which M^r Sergeant Holloway knoweth of. To daughter Mary Wenman £1000. To Sir Grevill Verney, £1000 due from the estate of the late Lord Wenman. The said Mary to have her legacy when married or when 18. Son Phillipp £50 in broad gold, and the gold left him by his mother sealed up in a paper. To daughters Dorothy and Mary two similar parcels of gold, they to be guided by their brother Richard, who has made up their portions to £3000. My estate to pass to my son Richard. To Mary, wife of Thomas Smith, a messuage in Wittney, late in the tenure of Abraham Bergo, deceased, during her life, if she pay Sarah Bergo, widow, £5 annually, and a chief rent of 3s. to my son. Poor of Wittney £10. Servants Edward Martindale, Walter Payn and John Sellary, £10 each. To Richard Beerley and John Acres 20s., Abraham Smith £5, John Eackly 40s., and Eliz. Quinney and Joane Smith a year's wages. Son Richard to be sole Executor and Tutor of his brother and sisters.

Witnesses: Richard Holloway, Rich. Lydall, James Almont.

Proved 4 Oct. 1680 by Richard. (Bath, 136.)

GREGORY WEAMAN (Weyman in will) of Birmingham, Baker.

1 Feb., 2 Jas. II. (1686).

Soul to God. Body to be decently buried. To my 5 younger children Thomas, John, Elizabeth, Anne and Mary, all my messuage or tenement and garden in Birmingham, in occupation of Wm. Law, Jun., and 3 closes of land (lately made 5), part of the Priors Connyzgree, bought of Wm. Pickard, and 3 other closes belonging to the same messuage towards Walmore lane, and 7 messuages and a barn at the lower end of Leays Lane, shooting into Edgbaston Street, and all others of which I hold fee simple. To hold the same for 99 years. Eldest son William to pay the said children, until 21, the sum of £160 and £5 each at Michelmas for their maintenance. If this be performed, the said messuages to be his. Wife Elizabeth to have an annuity of £20, with power of distress for non-payment. Son William all personal estate, he and my wife to be executors.

Witnesses: Rich. Bakwell, Edw. Capps, John Orton, Will. Greene, Sam. Eden.

Proved at London 2 May 1687 on oath of Elizabeth and William. (Foot, 70.)

SIR RICHARD WENMAN, Viscount WENMAN of Tuam, of Caswell, co. Oxon.

22 Oct. 1689.

The custody and guardianship of my younger children, viz., son Richard and daughters Katherine and Mary, to Katherine my wife until they come of age. To each of them £10,000 when 21. In case of the death of one daughter her share to be paid to the survivor. Wife to be Executrix, and to sell tenements in Hampton Gay, co. Oxon, and elsewhere, bought of Mr. Vincent Barrys, to pay my debts and funeral expenses. My lands in Ensham, co. Oxon, bought of Mr. Edgerley, in like manner, if need there be. Lease of the Rectory of Twiford, held of Lincoln College, Oxon, to be renewed, being requisite to my Estate there and elsewhere in Bucks.

Witnesses: Mark May, Thos. Tringham, Walter Powell.

Proved at London 8 July 1691 by Lady Catherine the relict. (Vere, 125.)

MARY, wife of GERRARD WEYMANS of London, Merchant (By virtue of marriage articles dated 8 April 1659.)

8 July 1691.

Soul to God. To brother M$^r$ William Vanbrough £5. To Elizabeth Vanbrough, widow of Giles Vanbrough, £5. To Susanna Nicolls, Sarah Bouchery and Mary Cooke, £5 each. That £3000, after the death of M$^r$ Gerrard Weymans, my husband, be paid to Mr. Jaspar Vanderbush alias Deloe and Anne his wife, to their use during life, and to their children after their decease, together with the household goods at my disposal, which I give after my husband's death to the said Jaspar. The remainder I leave, whether lands or property, to my husband, whom I make executor.

Witnesses: John Reynolds, Peter Deloe, Jane Nubery.

Licence granted to Jaspar Vanderbush to administer. Dated, Port Royal, Jamaica, 7 Jan. 1702. (Ash, 122.)

### Philip Wenman of Casswell, co. Oxon, Esq.
#### 6 Feb. 1692.

Soul to God. Sister M$^{rs}$ Doralisa Smith £2500, being part of £6000 due to me from my brother Viscount Wenman, deceased. To my sister M$^{rs}$ Mary Roberts the like. To my sister-in-law Viscountess Wenman £20 for mourning. To cousin M$^r$ Edmund Fettiplace of Swinbrook £20. To my brother-in-law M$^r$ Richard Smith £20, and all my horses, mares, and colts, beseeching him to keep my bay gelding as long as he live. Brother-in-law M$^r$ Gabriel Roberts £20. To M$^r$ Thomas Brooke a hundred guineas. Servant Joseph Colins £10. Poor of Whitney £10. To my two sisters Doralissa and Mary my estate at Mainewen, Caermarthen, to be divided between them.

Witnesses: Ferdinando Shepard, Walter Cotten, Henry Jones.

5 Feb. 1728, commission to Philip Roberts and Richard Smith, nephews on the sister's side and next-of-kin, to administer. (Abbott, 61.)

### John Wiman of Langley Marish, co. Bucks, Carpenter.
#### 12 April 1695.

Soul to God. Body to the earth. Copyholds in Iver to my son Robert Wiman for life, and after his death to the heirs of his body, but failing issue, to my son Henry and my three daughters Elizabeth Pitt, Mary Langley, and Martha Smith. To my wife Elizabeth a freehold messuage in Iver called Lew Croft during her life, with remainder to my son Robert. My freehold messuage in Langley Marrish, now in the possession of Jonathan Fellowes, to son Robert. Cottage in that place to wife for life. To grandson Henry, 2$^d$ son of my son Henry, the interest in certain copyholds in Upton, near Chalway, co. Bucks, now in possession of my son-in-law Robert Pitt, which I hold during the life of Jeptha Huntley, to my five grandchildren, sons and daughters of the said Robert Pitt. To daughter Martha Smith £100, and to her children 50s. each. To son Henry £10, and 50s. each to his children, and to the children of Mary Langley the like. To my wife Elizabeth household goods, etc. To Elizabeth Taylor her daughter £5, and to her daughters

Dorothy Judge and Sarah Skillman 20s. each. To Charles Daw of Langley, gent., 20s. for a ring. To James Bennett, formerly my apprentice, 40s. To the poor of Langley Marish 40s. Executor, son Robert.

Witnesses: Charles Dawe, John Turner, Richard Tudor.

Proved at London 27 June 1695 by Robert the son. (Irby, 108.)

### Gerrard Weymans of London, Merchant.
### 8 Oct. 1695.

Soul to God. Kinsman M$^r$ Jasper Vandenbush of All Hallowes the Less, Merch$^r$, living in Thames Street, all my goods, chattles and Estate in trust; to see my body buried, and pay debts and legacies. He to be Executor. (No legacies mentioned.)

Proved 3 Feb. 1700 by Jaspar.

Note.—4 Aug. 1709 Letters of administration granted to Anne, relict of Jaspar Vanden Bush. (Dyer, 30.)

### Daniel Weyman of Gloucester, gent.
### 12 Dec. 1696.

Soul to God. Body to the earth. To kinswoman Sarah Cartwright of Gloucester, widow, and Thomas Hawkins of Hardwick, co. Gloucester, yeoman, all interests in Copyhold Estate at Longney, co. Glouc., called Agashills, to be divided between them. To kinsman Henry Haywood £10 to set him up in the world when out of his apprenticeship. To kinswoman Anne Cleavely, widow, £20. If Henry Haywood die, his legacy to pass to Anne Cleavely the younger. The parties first above-named to be executors.

Witnesses: Paul Harding, Anne Walker, Nath$^l$ Lye, jun.

Proved 25 June 1697. (Pyne, 131.)

### Samuel Weyman of St. Olaves, Southwark, Felmonger.
### 20 March 1699.

Soul to Almighty God. Body to the earth at Clift, co. Nthts. £20 for funeral. To wife Elizabeth £100, to be paid her seven years after my death if she keep a widow, in the meantime to be put out in trust, she to receive the interest. To my four children John, Samuel, Joseph and Elizabeth Joane, the said £100 on mother's death. Household plate, etc., to wife during widowhood. If she marry again, to be divided among the children. To John £100. To son Samuel lands in Clift bought of M<sup>r</sup> Lewis of Bennifield, and £100 when 21. Son Joseph messuage in Clift bought of M<sup>r</sup> Bell, and £100. Daughter Elizabeth £200 at marriage or 21. If she die her legacy to be divided between John, Samuel and Joseph, her brothers. Executors: wife, M<sup>r</sup> George Waite of Clift, maltster, and John Bowden of the same, farmer.

Witnesses: Richard Ewer, Ann Roaper, Edward Knowles, Notary Public of Bermondsey Street, Southwark.

Proved 28 April 1701 on oath of Elizabeth the relict. (Dyer, 56.)

FRANCIS WEYMAN of London, merchant and scarlet dyer.

18 July 1700.

Living at Foxhall, co. Surrey, in Lambeth. Soul to Almighty God. Body where it please executors. Debts and duties to be paid. To M<sup>r</sup> Peter Scrieber of London, Merch<sup>t</sup> and Scarlett dyer, £50 for a ring, and the whole of "our in comon being household stuffe and furniture," nothing thereto relateing excepted the lands and tenements I have in Diepenfens, Linc., soe as it is now administred by my Brother M<sup>r</sup> John Weymans and my brother in law The Rev<sup>d</sup> D<sup>r</sup> Henry Lee, one part of which I leave to the said John and his heirs, and the other to the said Henry, and all the residue of my goods (except £800 I keep to be disposed of as I direct). My sister M<sup>rs</sup> Sibilla Weymans, wife of M<sup>r</sup> William de Meij, Councillor at Law, living in Rotterdam, are entirely excluded. Brother John and Peter Screiber Executors with D<sup>r</sup> Lee.

Witnesses: M<sup>r</sup> Francis Weyman, Wm. Woollhead, Rob<sup>t</sup> Heminway, Philip de Cole, Notary Public.

Proved at London 3 Nov. 1701 by Executors. (Dyer, 162.)

JANE WENMAN of Little Bath Street in St. James's, Clerkenwell, co. Mdx., widow.

(No date.)

Debts and funeral expenses to be paid. Residue to daughter Jane Theodosius Wenman. Executor, Alexander Anderson of Princes Street, Lothbury, Esq.

Witnesses: R. W. Clarkson, Margaret Jackson.

Proved at London 11 Nov. 1708 by the said executor. (Golding, 566.)


NICHOLAS WAYMAN of Loweastof, co. Suffolk, Marriner.

14 Jan. 1703.

Soul to God and my Body to the Earth or Sea. All such tickets, wages, pay and other estate to my dear and honoured father, Francis Wayman of the same place, Marriner. Exec. my trusty friend Robert Briggs of S$^t$ John, Wapping, or Ann his wife.

Witnesses: James Young, Anthony White, Will$^m$ Launam, Notary Public.

Proved at London 20 July 1711 by Rob$^t$ Briggs.


MARTHA WENMAN of Norwich, widow.

29 June 1710.

Soul to God, to be buried at discretion of my executor. All personal estate, plate and my own picture to my daughter Deborah Decelee my Executrix.

Witnesses: Eliz. Taylor, Eliz. Clayton.

Proved at London 11 Feb. 1713 by Deborah, wife of Samuel Decelee, the daughter. (Aston, 42.)


SAMUEL WEYMAN, Surgeon, of "the 'Dover' Galley of Bristol."

4 July 1716.

I committ and commend my soule into the hands of Almighty God. My body (in case of my decease in England) to be decently interred. To my sister Elizabeth Weyman of St. Mary Magdalen, Bermondsea, all goods, moneys, Bonds, my debts and funeral expenses first paid. Eliz^th to be executrix.

Witnesses: George Isaacke, John Dalby, Jos. Collyer.

Proved 8 Oct. 1717 by Elizabeth, sister of deceased.

### THOMAS WAYMAN of H.M.S. "Norwich."
### 8 June 1719.

Soul to God. All to my mother Dorothy Carpenter of All Hallowes Barkin, London, she to be executrix.

Witnesses: Robert Brodley, John Roades, Stephen Bellas, scrivener, near the Navy Office.

Proved at London 16 Aug. 1720 by Dorothy the relict. (Shaller, 186.)

### WILLIAM WAYMAN.
### 13 April 1720.

Forgives brother James Laxon a small debt. To sister Elizabeth Laxson £10. To kinsman Jonas Coal Laxson £10. To kinswoman Elizabeth Laxson £40. To sister Anne Willgras £10. Forgives brother Joseph Willgras a debt of £12. Kinswoman Elizabeth Willgras £40. Kinsmen John and William Corlenes £10 each. To Elizabeth Meler £40. Residue to Jonas Willgras, my executor. To William Gray, Elizabeth Gray, and William Apelyard a guinea each.

Witnesses: W^m and Eliz. Gray, William Apelyerd.

Proved at London 27 April 1720 by Jonas Willgrass. (Shaller, 97.)

### KATHERINE WEYMANS of St. Martin in the Fields, co. Mdx., widow.
### 11 June 1723.

I resign my soul etc. My Body I committ to the earth to be decently interred in the same grave with my late dear friend M^rs Lucretia Gilmore, near the tomb of my dear mother M^rs Mary Harris, in Camberwell churchyard. To cousin Anne Halford, my dear uncle Holland's da., £10 for mourning and a ring worth 20s. Her little son £100, to be laid out at interest in some Government Fund. If he die the sum to be paid his mother. M^rs Duke, wife of M^r Charles Duke, all my silver plate, my pearl necklace of two rows,

and to their da. Anne, my god-dau., my pearl necklace
of one row, my earrings, and £500. My Friend M^r James
Albin, £10 for his great care of me in sickness. My dau.
Miller, seven guineas for mourning and a ring worth 20s.
M^r Cole, M^rs Vanberham's niece, £10, M^rs Iremonger £5
and a ring, M^rs Hewston £5 and a ring. My aunt Holland,
her son, and her dau. Powell, my Lady Shaw, my cousin
Paggon and my cousin Morris, a ring worth 20s. Friends
M^rs Grove, M^rs Carr, M^rs Hall, M^r Albin, M^r Burke,
M^r Walker, M^rs Browne, M^rs Martin, M^rs Bowman,
M^rs Saunders, M^rs Smith and M^r Hawkins, rings. God-
daughter Miss Carr a peece of plate worth £15, my maid
Susan Benson all wearing apparell and linen and £15, £5
for mourning, my great Bible and a ring. To Lydia,
M^rs Browne's maid, a ring. To the poor housekeepers of
Camberwell £10. Residue to M^r Charles Duke, Executor.
Overseer, M^r John Llewellyn, to whom I give £40, and £10
for mourning.

Witnesses: Mary Arbrough, Margaret Arbrough and
Mainwaring Davies.

Proved at London 1 July 1723 by Charles Duke.
(Richmond, 156.)

EDWARD WINMAN of Chiswick, Mdx., gent.

5 Oct. 1724.

Soul to God. Body to be buried in the churchyard of
Chiswick. Debts and Funeral expenses to be paid. To
nephew Thomas Cobb of S^t Martin in the Fields, Baker,
messuage in S^t Alban's Street in S^t James, Westminster,
in occupation of M^r Didier, Surgeon, after the death of
Anne my wife. To niece Ann Siples of Easton Mauditt,
co. Nthts., £50. To nephew Richard Tongue of Rothwell,
Nthts., butcher, £40. To Mary his wife £40. Godson
Edward Tongue £50. To Hannah his sister, daughter of
Richard and Mary, £40. To Gerrard her brother £40.
My wife's godson Richard Tongue, their brother, £40.
To Thomas his brother £40. To my goddaughter Eliza-
beth, daughter of Robert Cobb, late of St. Giles in the
Fields, baker, £20. To James, son of James and Mary
Brittain, pewterer, £10. To Ann [*blank*], daughter of
Thomas Crawford of Whitefriars, porter, £20. To servant
Ann Mead £60. To Sibella, wife of John Richardson

of S$^t$ James, Westminster, blacksmith, £30. To Ann their daughter £20. To Norway Huton, now clerk to M$^r$ Holmes, soapmaker of Westminster, £10. To Ann Huton his mother £5. To Mary, daughter of Richard Wallis of S$^t$ Margaret's, Westminster, labourer, £10. To Mary Holmes of S$^t$ Martin in the Fields, widow of Edward Holmes, £20. To Joseph Cook, apprentice to Thomas Cobb, £10. The above to be discharged after the death of my wife. To Elizabeth, wife of Thomas Cobb, baker, £10 for mourning and a guinea for a ring. Richard Tongue and his wife, rings. The like to M$^r$ Dormer and his wife, and my cousin Christian Smith. To the poor of Chiswick £5. To Richard Graves, gent., of S$^t$ James, Westminster, £10 for mourning. Residue to my wife, whom I make Executrix with Thomas Cobb and Richard Graves.

Witnesses: Anne and John Snook, and Elizabeth Ladiman their servant.

Proved 14 Oct. 1725 by Ann the widow. (Romney, 222.)

### Richard Wiyman of Wilsdon, Middx.
### 30 Aug. 1727.

Soul to God. Body to be buried in Christian manner. To my father Thomas Wiyman of Broomfeild, Salop, £50. Cousin Jeremy, son of John Berry of S$^t$ Anne, Soho, £100. Wife Mary, all real estate in Wilsdon and house in Portugal St., S$^t$ James, and 2 Houses in High Park Corner, one in possession of John Jones, the other of Christopher Gundre, to hold them for life, with remainder to the lawful children of my brother Thomas Wayman and my sister Ann Berrey's children and my sister Margaret Hocking's children. Wife executrix.

Witnesses: Henry Little, Edmund Franklyn, Jn. Lewis. (Bedford, 27.)

### John Waymon of St. Botolph without Aldgate, London.
### 20 Nov. 1727.

Soul to God. Body to the earth. Wages, money, goods and chatells to wife Isabella Waymon. She to be Executrix.

T.: John Waterson, Edw. Westall, Tho. Parr, Scr.

Proved 2 May 1739 by Isabella. (Henchman, 119.)

ANNE WINMAN of Chiswick. Relict of EDWARD WINMAN, deceased.

22 April 1728.

Soul to God. Body by Husband. Debts and funeral expenses to be paid. To M<sup>rs</sup> Elizabeth Brawne of Covent garden, spinster, £10. To M<sup>rs</sup> Jane Brawne, her sister, £10. To Sibella Richardson, wife of John Richardson, smith, £10. To Anne Philpott, daughter of Thomas Crawford of White Fryars, porter, £10. To godson Richard, son of Richard Tongue of Rothwell, butcher, £10. To Edward, son of Edward Holmes, souldier, £10. To Ann Mead my servant, £100 in lieu of the £60 left her by my husband, to be laid out in an annuity for her use, she to have my large Bible, the Blue bed, bedding, etc. To M<sup>r</sup> Henry Palmer of Russell Street, Covent garden, a silver tobacco box. To Mary Miller my servant, £5. To nephew Thomas Cobb and his wife, M<sup>r</sup> Alden and his wife of Covent garden, The Rev<sup>d</sup> M<sup>r</sup> Wood of Chiswick, M<sup>r</sup> Dormer and his wife, M<sup>rs</sup> Elinor Sunclide, M<sup>r</sup> Richard Graves, gent., a guinea each for rings. Residue to Thomas Cobb and Richard Graves the Executors.

Witnesses: John and Anne Snooke, Catherine Hentley, nurse to M<sup>rs</sup> Palmer.

Proved at London 6 June 1728 by the Executors. (Brooke, 19.)

JACOB WAYMAN, Master of H.M.S. "The Dolphin."

22 July 1728.

Soul to God. Body to the earth or sea. All property, Lands, tenements, goods, chatels, wages, etc., to wife Joane Wayman of Waymouth, whom I appoint Executrix.

Witnesses: Margaret Joyce, William Thompson, Charles Power, Scrivener and freeman of London.

Commission 4 Nov. 1731 to Anne, wife and attorney of Edward Kirby, principal creditor of testator, of H.M.S. "Le Larke" and attorney of Edward her husband in parts beyond the Sea. Joane the widow renouncing. (Isham, 293.)

### William Weayman of Birmingham.

#### 30 March 1730.

To wife and her heirs a messuage and lands in Derby, Darley, and Morton, co. Derby, which were hers before her marriage, with £200, and all the jewels, rings, plate, etc., she brought with her, in lieu of any further claim. To the Charity School in Birmingham £200. Residue to brother Thomas Weaman, he to be exec$^r$.

Witnesses: Mary Bunton, Hannah Field, and Tho. Perks.

Proved 10 July 1730 by Thomas. (Auber, 227.)

### William Wymant.

#### 22 Dec. 1730.

There is £21 in M$^r$ Abbott's hand, of which to M$^{rs}$ Catherine Flood of Great Raynham, co. Norf., £5 5s. Residue to my sister Mary Wymant of Glaton, co. Hunts, she to bury me.

On 24 Dec. 1733 appeared Robert Abbott of S$^t$ Margaret's, Westminster, brewer, and Catherine Gerrard of S$^t$ James, Westminster, spinster, and swore on oath they knew William Wymant of S$^t$ George's, Hanover Square, the one for 20 years, the other for 2, and that they believe the paper was wholly written by deceased.

Power granted 24 Dec. 1733 to Mary Henson alias Wymant, wife of William Henson and sister of deceased, to administer the goods of deceased. (Price, 325.)

### Thomas Weyman, Mariner, H.M.S. "Tyger."

#### 3 July 1732.

All pay, wages, tickets, sums of money, lands, etc., to wife Francis, she to be Exec$^x$.

Witnesses: H. Crooks, Jasper Foster, Clerk.

Proved at London 11 Jan. 1742. (Boycott, 27.)

## WAYMAN WILLS.

EVA WAYMAN of Spalding, widow of JOHN WAYMAN, gent., now living with my daughter HELENA WEYMAN of Red Lion Street, London, spinster.
### 24 Dec. 1733.

All my lands at Swineshead, co. Linc. and elsewhere, late in the occupation of Henry Watson, to Helena Wayman my daughter, whom I make executrix, but she is not to sue John Wayman my son for rent out of my messuage in Spalding, wherein he dwells. The executors of my late son Cornelius Wayman are released from any claims due to me.

Witnesses: Bridget Hutchinson, Mary Barker, Henry B. Lacey.

Proved at London 17 Dec. 1736 by Helena. (Derby, 284.)

ELIZABETH WYMAN of Walthamstow, co. Essex, singlewoman.
### 15 June 1734.

To be buried at discretion of my Executrix. To cousins Anne Pitt and Elizabeth Ladbrooke of Upton, co. Bucks, all my money in trust to maintain my mother Elizabeth Wyman for life, with remainder to my said cousins. To my cousins my trunk in keeping of M<sup>r</sup> Francis Winfield of Iver, and all therein. To Mary Lambeth, servant to Edward Conyers, Esq., of Walthamstow, my Calamanta gown and old stays. To Mary Smith her fellow servant my cotton gown. Residue to Anne Pitt and Elizabeth Ladbrooke my executors.

Witnesses: Elizabeth Yallop, Joseph Eyre.

Proved 3 July 1734 by Elizabeth Ladbrooke. (Ockham, 171.)

ROBERT WAINMAN, Mariner, of H.M.S. "Defiance."
### 17 March 173⅚.

Soul to God. Body to the earth or sea. Wearing apparell and bedding to friend and shipmate William Williamson. Lands, tenements, goods, etc., to father Samuel Wainman my executor.

Witnesses: Charles Evans, Humphrey Woodman, Captain's Clerk.

Commission 1 June 1737 to William Wainman, attorney of Samuel Wayman of Scalby, co. York, the father of deceased. (Wake, 148.)

MARY WAYMAN of Wilsden, Middlesex, widow.

30 May 1738.

My soul I commend to God. Debts and funeral charges to be paid. Sister-in-law Martha Page, widow, who lives with me, £20. Friend W$^m$ Johnson of S$^t$ James, Westminster, butcher, £20. Elizabeth his wife, my gold watch, chain and seal. Mary Brooks of Edgware, Midd$^x$, widow, £20. Cousin Mary, wife of [blank] Watson, £20, to her own use. Cousin Hannah Parrett of Rickmonsworth, spinster, £10. Martha, da. of Tho. Page, late of the Haymarket, spinster, wearing apparel and clothes, etc., to her, together with Martha, da. of W$^m$ Page deceased, Martha Page, widow beforesaid, and Martha, wife of John Carter of Wilsden, salesman, to be shared between them. The said Martha, da. of W$^m$ and Martha Page, diamond ring. My servant Rich$^d$ Paine, all Freeholds in Wilsden. My sister-in-law Martha Page, the leaseholds there for life, remainder to Martha her da. Remaining Estate to Cousin George Nicholl of Southwark, hatter, and Eliz$^{th}$, w. of [blank] Nott of Southwark, Stowterer, Martha, da. of W$^m$ and Martha Page, and their heirs.

Exec$^{rs}$: W$^m$ Johnson and Martha Page.

Proved 27 Sept. 1741 by Martha Page, widow. (Spurway, 247.)

THOMAS WAYMAN of Darts Alley in Whitechappel, of H.M.S. "Wager."

12 Aug. 1740.

To wife Elizabeth 2 houses in Harwich, and all wages, goods, chattels and estate, she to be executrix.

Witnesses: Daniel Kidd, Capt., Peter Denis, Lieut.

Proved at London 14 June 1746. (Edmunds, 195.)

ROBERT WIMAN of Langley March, co. Bucks, carpenter.
16 Nov. 1741.

To son Robert Wiman a messuage in Langley March formerly Jonathan Felloeo's, and all freeholds in Iver called Lowcrofts, but he is charged to pay my son Henry Wiman £20, and my daughter Elizabeth, the wife of William Thurbin, the like, but if she die within 12 months of my decease, to her children. To son John, my silver tankard and gold ring, wife Mary to dwell in my house a whole year after my death, and her provision supplied to her free of cost, she to have £12 and certain bedding, and the furniture in the chamber over the parlour, and all the linen she brought with her. To son Henry a gold ring. Residue to son Robert, my executor, to pay my debts and funeral expenses.

Witnesses: Elizabeth and William Brookland and John Spurr.

Proved at London 19 Sept. 1743 by Robert, son and Executor. (Boycott, 300.)

SUSANNAH, LADY VISCOUNTESS DOWAGER WENMAN.
14 June 1742.

Soul to God. Body to earth. Everything to son Richard Wenman, he to pay debts. £20 for mourning to M<sup>rs</sup> Bainton my companion. Cloathes, etc., to my woman. Son Richard to be Executor.

Witnesses: Mary Littleton, William Clark, Charles Pryor.

Proved at London 28 Feb. 1750 by Richard. (Busby, 67.)

HENRY WIMAN of Mercer's Court in Tower Street, Bricklayer.
21 Oct., 17 George II.

Soul unto Almighty God. Body at discretion of my Executrix. All estate to wife Katherine, she to be executrix.

Witnesses: Blissett Wooddeson, Tho<sup>s</sup> Gooscott.

Proved at London 26 Oct. 1743 by Katherine. (Boycott, 327.)

JOSIAH WAYMAN, Surgeon's Mate on H.M.S. "Roebuck."
11 June 1744.

Soul to God. All beds, bedding, linnen, etc., to my father, Rev. Lewis Wayman of Kimbolton, co. Hunts.

Witnesses: J. Barnes, H. Edw$^d$ Gibson.

Proved at London 14 June 1748 by Lewis the father of deceased. (Strahern, 198.)


GEORGE WAYMAN of H.M.S. "Wager."
2 Dec. 1744.

Soul to God. Body to earth. All wages, tenements, goods, etc., to mother Joane Wayman of S$^t$ Paul's, Deptford, co. Kent. She to be executrix.

Witnesses: Sam$^l$ Lofting, John Fowley, W$^m$ Goagh.

Proved at London 11 June 1764 by Joane. (Simpson, 247.)


MATHEW WENMAN of London Bridge in St. Olave, Southwark, Coffee Man.
26 Dec. 1744.

Soul to God. To be buried in the part of the churchyard belonging to S$^t$ Olave. Debts and funeral expenses to be paid. To father and mother Joseph and Susannah Wenman £5 each. Sister Susannah Wenman £5. Brother Joseph the like. Richard his son one shilling. Brother Amos a guinea for a ring. Elizabeth his wife the like. Charles their son a guinea. Brother-in-law Peter Johnson of Cookham, co. Berks, Labourer, £5. Sarah his wife £5. Sarah their daughter £10. Ann her sister £5. Mary her sister the like. Henry her brother £5. Joseph his brother £5. Mathew his brother 1$s$. To my maid Hannah Sealy £20. To Thomas Barnes of Gray's Inn, gent., my late master, a guinea for a ring. To Robert Boxton of Fetter Lane, gent., and his wife the like. To Mary Biddle, niece of Robert Boxton, a ring. Residue to brother Henry Wenman my executor.

Witnesses: George Thurlow, William Adams, Martha Warne.

Proved at London 5 Feb. 1749 by Henry. (Greenly, 63.)

JACOB WAYMAN of Weymouth and of Melcombe Regis, co. Dorset.

26 Jan., 20 George II.

Soul to God. Body to the earth. All pay, wages and Estate to wife Susanna the Executrix.
Witnesses: Nath¹ Allen, W<sup>m</sup> Penney, James Gair.
Proved at London 24 May 1748. (Strahan, 168.)


WILLIAM WENMAN, Esq., of Edwinstowe, co. Notts.

3 Jan. 1749.

Soul to God. To Cavendishe, Countess of Oxford, and her heirs my Estate at Harley in Clifton, co. Notts, bought of Francis Brown, and £500. To George Mason of Eaton, Esq., and Abell Smith, Junior, Banker, my estates in Edwinstowe, Laneham, Dunham and Mansfield Woodhouse, co. Notts, in trust to pay my wife Ellen the issues and rents during her life, and after her death to convey my Estate in Edwinstowe to William Cavendish Bentinck, Marquis of Titchfield, and his heirs, together with all my paintings, prints, looking-glasses, and the chairs and furniture of my best parlour, and the coppers, brewing vessels, etc., in my house at Edwinstowe. To my nephew William Wenman my estate in Mansfield Woodhouse. My estates in Laneham and Dunham to be sold by the said trustees, and after the expenses, etc., deducted, the remainder to be divided among the children of my late brother the Rev<sup>d</sup> George Wenman. By deed dated June 1711 I set aside with John Farr, my wife's brother, now living, and Henry Farr, her uncle, long since dead, £900 to the use of myself, my wife and children. And whereas we have only one daughter, Margaret Heartley, who in a very unkind and indiscreet manner disposed of herself in marriage to one M<sup>r</sup> Abel Bartley, without our consent or approbation, I desire in lieu my trustees to deduct from my estate £1,200 and pay the interest to my daughter during life, as I do not desire she should want bread, and invest it in Chancery for the benefit of her child or children. If the said Abel refuse the conditions, the sum to pass, half to John Farr, half the children of my brother George. My printed books to be placed in the Library at

Welbeck after my wife's death. To the poor of Edwinstowe £10. The poor of Cuckney £10. My wife to be Executrix. Funeral to be private, without the Ceremony of Pall Bearers.

Witnesses: John Simes, John Dakeyne, John Gladwin.

*Codicil*, dated 4 Jan. 1749. Revoking legacy of £500 to the Countess of Oxford, etc., and at her command charging the Estate at Edwinstowe with £1,200 to the use of the children of George Wenman.

Witnesses as above.

*Codicil*, dated 27 March 1750. Specifically leaving plate to wife, viz., a large waiter and 2 large sauce boats, weighing 47 oz. 6 dr., to her own use and disposal, a large silver cup and cover given me by my mother, a silver chased jug, 2 salts and spoons, to go after my wife's death to my nephew William Wenman. Certain other silver plate to niece Ann Wenman.

Proved at London 15 Dec. 1750. (Greenly, 406.)

ANN WAINMAN of St. Paul, Shadwell, co. Middlesex, widow.

8 June 1751.

Debts and funeral expenses to be paid. To daughter Ann my house held of Edward Gilbert, Esq., in Shadwell, and all wearing apparel. To son Thomas Wainman copyhold on Cockhill in Ratcliffe, called the "George" alehouse. Residue between my son and daughter. Executrix and friend M<sup>rs</sup> Mary Glover of Royston.

Witnesses: William Martin, Margaret Apthorp.

Proved at London 26 July 1751 by Mary Glover, spinster, executrix. (Busby, 227.)

THOMAS WAINMAN of Ratcliff Highway in the parish of St. Paul's, Shadwell, haberdasher.

20 Sept. 1754.

Debts and Funeral expenses to be paid. All real and personal estate to M<sup>rs</sup> Mary Glover, Executrix.

Witnesses: W<sup>m</sup> Porter, Barbara Porter, and Ann Hewllings.

Proved at London 6 Feb. 1758 by Mary Glover. (Hulton, 58.)

## WAYMAN WILLS.

JOHN WENMAN, mariner, of H.M.S. "Orford," Captain Richard Spry.
3 March 1757.

Soul to God. Body to the earth or sea. To wife Mary of St. Clements [Ipswich], co. Suffolk, all lands, tenements, goods, etc.

Witnesses: James Walker, William Addamson.

Proved 30 Oct. 1758 by Mary the widow. (Hulton, 317.)

ELLEN WENMAN of Edwinstow, co. Notts.
2 Dec. 1757.

All goods, etc., and personal estate to friends, George Mason of Eaton, Esq., and Abel Smith of Nottingham, Esq., in trust to dispose of the same to the use of the children of my late daughter Margaret, wife of Abel Bartley deceased. To the poor of Edwinstow and Cuckney £10, that is £5 to each parish.

Witnesses: Ann Castmeat, Allice Wilson, John Whitaker.

Proved at London 9 March 1765 by the Executors, George Mason and Abel Smith. (Rushworth, 125.)

JOHN WIMAN of Iver alias Ever, co. Bucks, Yeoman.
21 April 1758.

Soul to God. Body to the earth. To brother Robert copyhold lands in Iver, viz., 22 acres with their appurtenances, but not to take full possession until the mortgage thereon be paid off. Housekeeper Sarah Carr 50s. Residue to brother Robert. Executors: William Bunyan, Junior, and my sister Elizabeth Wiman.

Witnesses: William Johnson, Thomas Butler, John Spencer.

Proved at London 5 June 1758 by Elizabeth, wife of Robert Wayman, one of the Executors. (Hulton, 204.)

PHILIP LORD WENMAN, Viscount Tuam.
4 May 1758.

Soul to my redeemer. To be buried at Twyford in a private manner, cost not to exceed £100. To George Hervey of Tiddington, Oxon, Esq., and Francis Bassett of

Walcutt, Esq., messuages, etc., at and near Whitney, Lands at Coggs and Brise Norton. The manor of Caswell and estate there worth £410 yearly. In trust to pay debts and legacies, and further to sell coppices and woods at Twyford and Caswell, and such estate as is limited to son Philip. Remaining estates in Oxford, Kent or Bucks to son Philip for life, and after determination of the estate by forfeiture or otherwise to Thomas Whorwood of Halton, co. Oxon, Esq., and John Clerke of Aston Rowant, Esq., in trust during the life of son Philip to preserve the contingent estates. The succession to pass to his eldest son, and if he die to his second son, and so forth in order of seniority, and the like during the life of my son Thomas Francis Wenman, and in default of heirs male, to my daughter Sophia and her heirs, and failing heirs, to my brother Richard Wenman and his heirs, and failing heirs, to my wife Sophia in like trust, and if she die without daughter or daughters, to her sister Miss Ann Herbert. Remainder to my right heirs. The estates to be charged in £2000 for the benefit of sons, daughter or daughters, viz., of Philip £1200, of Thomas Francis £800. If daughter's issue inherit, they to take name and arms of Wenman, and if their husbands refuse to procure an Act of Parliament, the Estate to pass to the next in remainder. Wife to have use of capital messuage called Thame Park with the plate, pictures and household goods therein, with certain lands about it, to make the same her chief residence, and on her death to son Philip, but if he die without male issue, to his brother, younger son or sons to be brought up to the sea or army, or in law, physick or divinity. Trustees to manage real estate till sons be 21. Wife to be guardian of daughter. Sister-in-law Ann to have £200 and all goods at Kingsey except the books, the picture of Philip, Earl of Pembroke, Sir Peter Lilly and his mistress, the picture of cocks and hens by Barlow, and another of dead game, which are to be considered to belong to Thame Park. Thos. Whorwood and John Clerke 20 guineas each, all servants half a year's wages and my cloaths and linnen. To servant Paul Mason an annuity of £10. To S$^t$ Bartholemews Hospital £100. Poor of Tame and Twyford £20 each. Executors: George Hervey and Francis Bassett, I give to them £100 each for mourning. Management of Estates to John Morton of Tackley. Residue to son Philip.

Witnesses: John and Edw. Vernon and George Hill.

*Codicil.* 17 May 1760. Deer to wife. The park to be disparked. M^rs Herbert to have the picture of the Earl of Pembroke if she wish. To James Blair £10 10s. To John Churchill Wickstead, Esq., 100 guineas for mourning. Brother Richard £20. M^r Richard Way of Thame £100, desiring him to be employed looking after the estate.

Witnesses: Robert Whalley, Thomas Brougham, Edward Rose.

*Codicil.* 12 July 1760. Desires to be buried at Thame Chapel in the park, and grave covered with marble with an inscription thereupon: Here lyeth the Body of Philip Lord Viscount Wenman, who was born Nov. 23, 1719, and died .... He married Sophia, daughter and coheiress of James Herbert, Esquire, of Tythorpe in the county of Oxford, by whom he had issue Philip the present Lord, born April 18, 1742. Sophia, born August 17, 1743. Susannah, born Nov. 10, 1744, who died young and was buried at Whitney. Thomas Francis, born Nov. 18, 1745. Richard, born Nov. 13, 1746, who died in his infancy and was buried at Whitney. Mary, born March 27, 1748, who died young and was buried at Whitney. And Herbert Henry, who also died young and was buried at Thame Park.

Pall bearers to be my servants, and £25 a year to be paid to some Minister to officiate at Thame Park.

Proved at London 14 Nov. 1760 by George Hervey, Esq. (Lynch, 447.)

## Ann Weaman of Birmingham.
## 14 March 1759.

Debts and funeral expenses to be paid. To the Charity School in Birmingham £400. To Mary, daughter of nephew Thomas Weaman, £700 out on a mortgage made by sister Felicia, deceased, on houses in Birmingham and Duddeston, and also £400. To James, son of Robert Hicks, deceased, son of my nephew William Hicks, £130. If he die under age, a third to Thomas son of my said nephew, a third to Alice sister of Thomas Hicks, a third to Hannah wife of Samuel Haines. To William, son of nephew William Hicks, an annuity when 50, viz., £15 yearly, and to Phebe his wife £10 yearly. To niece Alice

Leedham £5 and £15 yearly, and if she survive her sister Elizabeth Austin a further £5. To Alice Hicks £10 yearly. To Robert, son of nephew Tho. Hicks, £100. To the 5 children of nephew Gregory Hicks, William, Ann, Rebecca, Weaman and Felicia, £100 each. To Richard, Christopher and Elizabeth, children of nephew Christopher Hicks, £100. Mary, daughter of nephew Richard Hicks, £100, to the said Richard £500. Nephew Christopher to have 4 shillings a week for life and Elizabeth Austin £38 yearly. To Phebe and Anne, daughters of Hannah Haines, £20 each. Residue to nephews Thomas and Gregory Hicks. Desires to be buried in lead in a chapel in Birmingham.

Witnesses: Alice Cooper, Sarah Anderton, Tho. Steward.

Proved at London 21 Aug. 1759 by Tho. and Gregory. (Arran, 285.)

THOMAS WEYMAN of Llanguillo, co. Radnor, gent.
21 March 1760.

Three sons, John, Thomas and William in my care, as their mother is lately dead, of whom John is provided for under my marriage settlement. I bequeath to Richard Duppa of Culmington, Salop, gent., and William Smith of Peytoe in Leintwardine, co. Hereford, gent., my brothers-in-law, my messuage called The Raine of Bwlth in Clunn, co. Salop, and another at Bedoon, Salop, to raise £1,500 to pay my debts and provide for my sons Thomas and William, and all my personal estate in trust for my children to set them up in professions or trades. Also my messuage the Raine of Lower Weston in Llanguillo, bought by me of Jonas Vaughan, to be applied to the education of my said two sons. The Estate of Lower Weston to pass to my son John.

Witnesses: Joyce Meyrick, Jun., Edward Meyrick, Jun.

Proved at London 16 Feb. 1773 by Richard Duppa and Wm Smith, Executors. (Stevens, 87.)

JOSEPH WENMAN of Bray, co. Berks, Sheep Factor.
7 Feb. 1762.

All Personal estate to my brother John Wenman, Joseph Langton of Farnham, co. Bucks, yeoman, and

Richard Poulton of Sheephouse Farm, yeoman, in trust to continue at interest the sum of £800 and pay the same to my daughter Mary for her maintenance until she be 21, when the said Trustees shall transfer the sum or securities to her. Also to the said Mary the furniture in my best chamber, she to continue the sum of £1,100 standing in my name, and place out a further £200, to apply the same to clothe and educate her sisters Eadey and Sarah Wenman until 21, and to pay a moiety of the £200 to each. Also upon trust to pay my nephews and nieces, children of my sister Sarah, wife of Peter Johnson, such legacies as were given by my brother Matthew, deceased, and to my said sister Sarah £30. My servant Susanna Winter £50. And to my son Joseph Wenman (if all my daughters die) their several legacies. To place out the overplus of my personal estate, and apply the same for my son Joseph's education, etc. All freehold estate to my son and his heirs, failing issue to daughters, failing issue to brother John Wenman and his heirs. Executors: the three trustees.

Witnesses: William Sneath, Richard Simeon.

Proved at London 22 March 1762 by the executors. (St. Eloy, 135.)

SAMUEL WYMENT of Daventry, co. Northants, gent.

2 June 1762.

All household goods, etc., to wife Elizabeth, and £200 to be disposed of among her children. To my daughters Sarah and Elizabeth £500 each. Messuages, tenements, tithes, lands, etc., in Daventry and Drayton to wife for life, and after to James Warner of Westminster, gent., my kinsman, and William Rose of Daventry, gent., for 500 years in trust to raise £1000 for my daughters Sarah and Elizabeth, my daughter Mary Montgomery having already received £1000, and my daughter Catherine Harrison the like. After which the term of 500 years to cease, when all my estate shall pass to my four daughters to be divided equally between them.

Witnesses: John Oneley, Joseph Freeman, Thomas Jephcott.

Proved at London 12 May 1764 by Jas. Warner and Wm. Rose. (Simpson, 207.)

HENRY WENMAN of Fetter Lane in St. Andrew's, Holborne, gentleman.

### 9 Sept. 1762.

To be buried in the Fore Yard of S<sup>t</sup> Andrew's, Holborne, near the grave of Miss Batt, in a private manner. To Mary, daughter of Elizabeth Goodenough of Rainsbury, co. Wilts, 8 guineas. To my daughter Ann a silver pint mugg. Residue to daughters Ann Wenman and Martha Robinson, to be divided between them. Residue of personal estate to Ann.

Witnesses: John Needham, Thomas Dummer Parkes.

Proved at London 18 Sept. 1762 by Martha Robinson, widow. (St. Eloy, 407.)

AMOS WENMAN, Citizen and Haberdasher, of London.

### 16 March 1763.

Soul to God. To be buried at Cookham, co. Berks, in the vault I erected for my mother. Debts to be paid. To wife Elizabeth all my plate, watches, jewels, rings, linnen, goods in the house, etc., etc. Executors, brother John Wenman and Fenwick Lyddel, each to have £100. House and stock to be sold and invested, and from the interest wife to be paid £400 yearly for life, or as long as she remain a widow. To her son Charles Wenman £100 yearly. To my father £50 yearly during life, and to my sister Susannah Wenman the like. The sum of £25 yearly to be laid out for 98 years by the minister, churchwardens and overseers of Cookham in bread for the poor, to be distributed weekly in church, and the like to the minister, etc., of White Waltham, co. Berks, and the better to secure this £1762 shall remain in the Bank of England. Wife £20. Brother Richard a guinea, sister Sarah Johnson and her daughter £50 each, another daughter much afflicted in the eyes £50, their names I do not know. Maidservants £10 each, and the like to children of my brother John. Tenements at Langley Marsh and Bethnal Green and my 6th share of freeholds at Ormskirk, co. Lanc., to brother John and his wife for life, and after to their heirs.

Witnesses: Rob\* Holden, Henry Metcalfe, John Mazareen.

*Codicil.*—Revokes legacies to Charles his son and lands to his brother John. Gives wife another £100 annuity. To son Charles all his real estate. 17 March 1763.

Witnesses as above.

Administration granted 16 April 1763 of goods, etc., of Amos Wenman of S\* Bartholemew Exchange to Charles his son.

Proved at London 7 Feb. 1778. (Cæsar, 208.)


JOANE WAYMAN of St. Paul, Deptford.

15 March 1770.

Soul to God. Body to the earth. Executrix my cousin Sarah Bishop, Senior, to take all my goods, etc., and pay debts and funeral expenses, and divide them with John Leach.

Witnesses: John Creasy, Mary Collier. I cut off my grandson Isaac Wayman with a shilling, and desire grandson John Leach, Junr., shall have the great Bible.

Proved at London 19 July 1771 on oath of Sarah, wife of James Bishop. (Trevor, 325.)


JOHN WYMAN of Jewin Street in St. Giles, Cripplegate, in the City of London.

6 June 1772.

After payments of debts, funeral expenses and rings. Securities in 4 per cent. Consolidated Bank Annuities 1762 and furniture, etc., to wife Elizabeth for life, with remainder to my son Joseph. To John Smith of the "Adam and Eve" in Jewin Street £100 in trust for son Joseph. Apparel, linen and silver watch to son. Residue to be divided between my wife and son. To John Smith a guinea, and the like to my nephew John Platt and niece Elizabeth Bellamour for mourning. Executors, wife and John Smith.

Witnesses: John Prosser and W<sup>m</sup> Wood.

Proved at London 5 May 1780 by Elizabeth the relict. (Collins, 294.)

### Mary Wenman of Esher, co. Surrey, widow.
#### 1 Oct. 1772.

Debts and funeral charges to be paid. To Mary Sadler of Holbourn, widow, £100 in stock. If she die, to pass to her daughter Melicent Sadler, to whom I give £200 if she be living at my death. Also to her and her mother all household goods, furniture and apparel. To Mrs Ann Greaves of Richmond a five guinea piece. To John-George, son of John and Grace Felton of Holborne, £50. To Grace his mother the like. If John-George die under age his share to pass to his sister Margaret. To Grace Felton my gold watch and chain. To my cousin Henry Cox £15. To Mrs Sarah Alford a ring worth a guinea. To John Gould Floyer, Rector of Esher, £2 2s. in lieu of a scarfe, hatband and gloves. Copyhold in the manor of Aldwich is already conveyed to my kinsman Thomas Baker, surgeon. I desire my executor to confirm this. Residue to my first cousin John Baker, Esq., Barrister-at-Law, whom I appoint sole executor.

Witnesses: William and James Moore.
Proved 19 Dec. 1772 by the executor. (Taverner, 465.)

### Sophia, Viscountess Wenman.
#### 7 Feb. 1774.

Soul to God. To be buried by my husband in the chapel at Thame Park, cost of funeral not to exceed £100. My son Lord Wenman to be Executor and have £100 for the trouble, my earrings and the stars of my necklace, 3 drop earrings given me by my Lord's brother, and a large diamond given me by Lord Abington. To my daughter Sophia Wykham a bracelet, all my rings, little pictures and trinkets except those given to my son Thomas Francis Wenman, my plate and Motto snuffbox which was his father's. To sister Ann Herbert £100 and my gold French enamelled snuffbox. To my brother Richard Wenman £20. To the poor of Thame and Kingsey £20. All my cloaths to servant, except a new suit of Point I desire Mrs. Wykham to have. To my man five guineas and half a year's wages. Half a year's wages to all my servants. Residue between daughter Sophia Wykham and son Thomas Francis. To daughter Sophia three cases of silver knives and forks, the dessert spoons given me by M<sup>r</sup> Wykham, 1 Nov. 1781. To granddaughter Sophia Wykham my watch and seals and £20, and Harriot Wykham £20 and my gold chased smelling bottle and little Motto snuffbox. To Philip Wykham £20. The 28 Aug. 1781, Ann Allworthy of St. Mary le Bone, Mdx., gentlewoman, and Eleanor Ragsdell, spinster, made oath that they knew Sophia, Viscountess Wenman of Tythrop in Kingsey, co. Oxon, and declared the above will to be hers.

Affidavit sworn before George Harris, Surrogate, and R. Dodwell, Notary Public.

Proved at London 2 Aug. 1787 by Philip, Lord Wenman, son of deceased. (Major, 392.)

JOHN WHAYMAND, mariner, of H.M.S. "Panther."
28 Dec. 1777.

Soul to God. Body to earth or sea. All money, lands, goods, etc., to father John Whaymand of Ipswich, whom I appoint executor.

Proved at London 10 April 1783 by John, father of deceased. (Cornwallis, 206.)

WATSON WAYMAN of H.M.S. "Marlborough," Taylor Penny, Esq., Commander.
4 Aug. 1779.

Soul to God. Body to the earth or sea. All property to father Watson Wayman living in Union Lane, Sunderland.

Witnesses: Taylor Penny, Capt., Peter Kennedy.

Proved at London 5 March 1781 by Watson Waiman alias Wayman, father of deceased. (Webster, 173.)

HANNAH WAINMAN of Leeds, York.
17 April 1780.

Debts, etc., to be paid. To Martha Nettleton £5. To Henry Parkinson £1 1s. Residue to niece Jane Wainman, whom I appoint executrix.

Witnesses: Jacob Harrison, Thomas Harrison.

Proved at London 22 Aug. 1783 by Joane, wife of Henry Parkinson, neice of deceased. (Cornwallis, 440.)

JOHN WEYMAN, mariner, of the precinct of St. Catherine near the Tower, London.

1 Oct. 1780.

Soul to God. Body to earth or sea. All wages, money, etc., to wife Elizabeth, she to be sole executrix.

Witnesses: G. Farquharson, Howell Williams.

Proved at London 20 March 1792 by Elizabeth the widow. (Fountain, 186.)


WILLIAM WAYMAN, mariner, H.M.S. "Nonsuch."

2 Feb. 1781.

Soul to God. Body to the earth or sea. All pay money, wages, lands, etc., to Mark, Polly, Nancy and Susannah, my four children, to be equally divided between them. Executrix my wife Ann, if she die I appoint in her room William King of Hull, merchant.

Witnesses: T. Spry, 1st Lieut., Andrew Stone.

Commission to administer issued 16 Oct. 1783 to John Robinson, attorney of Ann the relict. (Cornwallis, 543.)


MARY WAINMAN of Esher.

23 April 1781.

Soul to God. Body to be decently buried. All property to husband William Wainman.

Witnesses: Mary Butler, Judith Jackson, Joseph Shwancenkruge.

Proved at London 3 May 1781 by William, husband of deceased.


DOROTHY WEAMAN of Sutton Coldfield, co. Warwick, widow.

11 July 1781.

My debts and funeral expenses to be paid. To Mary, widow of Edward Green, late of Johnson Hall, co. Staffs, Esq., £400. To Catherine, widow of the late Mr Daniel of

Colchester and daughter of my brother Edward Green of Lawford Hall, £50. To my friend Henry Kempson of Birmingham £20, as one of my executors. To Lucy Simmonds my servant £10 yearly for life, to be paid out of my leaseholds near St Mary's Chapel in Birmingham. To my executors £100 for such charitable purposes as they think fit and worthy. Residue to sister Mary Buchanan, she and Henry Kempson to be executors.

Witnesses: William Sanderson, George Hollington.

Proved at London 20 Oct. 1788 by Mary Buchanan, widow. (Calvert, 515.)

MATTHEW WYMAN of St. Saviour's, Southwark, Carpenter.

1 May 1782.

To my wife Margaret seven leasehold messuages in King Street for life, with remainder of the term to my son Matthew, both to fulfil the conditions set forth in the original lease. Paying my daughter Ann, wife of William Lawrence, £6 annually, and the like to my daughter Sarah, wife of John Hawkins, and a similar sum to my daughter Elizabeth, wife of Edward Parsons, and also an annuity of £10 to my son John. Residue to son and executor Mathew.

Witnesses: Nicholas Holding and H. Cross.

Proved at London 14 August 1782 by Mathew the son of deceased. (Gostling, 434.)

GEORGE WAYMAN of Cabinet Court, Duke Street, Old Artillery Ground in the Liberty of the Tower of London.

30 Nov. 1783.

Soul to God. Body to the earth. To Elizabeth Wayman my daughter, alias Gamage, my glass tankard with a silver cover and 2 guineas. My daughter Ann Wayman 2 guineas. My wife to be executrix, all household goods, linen, watch and wearing apparel and £50 in Bank annuities.

Witnesses: Henry Newberg, Jeremiah Simmons, Thomas Hutt.

Proved 26 January 1786 by the said wife Sarah. (Norfolk, 54.)

## WAYMAN WILLS.

CHRISTOPHER WYMAN of Walham Green in Fulham,
co. Mdx., Carpenter.

### 24 Aug. 1785.

To my wife Elizabeth Wyman my messuage at Walham Green, together with all my estate, she to pay £15 each to John, Thomas and George, my children, when 21. All household furniture, stock in trade, etc., to wife to pay my debts, she to be sole executrix.

Witnesses: Henry Ward, Oliver Stocker, Thomas Day.

Proved at London 5 Oct. 1785. (Ducarel, 533.)

ELIZABETH WYMAN of Jewin Street, London, widow.

### 18 Nov. 1786.

Debts, etc., to be paid. To son Joseph Wyman £100, in Four per cent. bank annuities. To my brother John Cook of Brick Lane, Old Street, co. Middlesex, £30, to be paid him by my executor Linstead Reeves of Hoxton, co. Middlesex, gent., by weekly payments of 4s., if he so long live. If he die, remainder at the discretion of M$^r$ Reeves, and Ann wife of the said John Cooks, to buy cloaths for her children. To Linstead Reeves a guinea for a ring. Remainder to my son Joseph Wyman.

Witnesses: Evan Owens, Edward Grose Smith, clerk to M$^r$ Wood in Nicholas Lane.

Proved at London 22 Nov. 1786 by Linstead Reeves, sole executor.

FRANCIS WYMAN of Stonebury in Little Hormead,
co. Hertford.

### 4 March 1789.

Soul to God. All estates owned as legatee of brother-in-law Edward Faircloth, gent., to eldest son William Wyman, £300, but if he receive the £500 due from my said brother-in-law, the £300 to be deducted therefrom and given to son William. To my daughter Catherine £600. To daughter Rose, wife of William Sworder, £300, as she has already received a marriage portion. To son Richard £800. To daughter Elizabeth £600. To daughter

Frances the like. To son Francis £800. To son George £900 when 24 years of age. Wife to find meat and drink, lodging, etc., until my children come of age. The farm at Stonebury to son Richard, but my wife to live there for a year. To brother-in-law Richard Warwick £15 if he assist my wife in the executorship. All my stock, etc., at Mutford's farm to wife, and a messuage at Stondon, co. Hertford, and the farm at Staustead Mountfitchet. To son Richard my moiety of lands in Stondon. To son Francis a messuage in Braughing and lands at Bromley in Stondon.

Witnesses: George Harkins and Tho. Mott, both of Much Hadham.

*1st Codicil.*—Revokes legacy to Richard as, owing to his marriage, he has been placed in possession. Son William and son-in-law William Sworder to be executors with my wife, together with Robert Warwick. Dated 28 March 1792.

Witnesses: Tho. Mott, W$^m$ Gorsuch-Times, George Starkins.

*2nd Codicil.*—Since my daughter Elizabeth is now wife of M$^r$ John Chapman and has received £300 of me, that sum to be deducted from her legacy. Dated 30 March 1792.

Witnesses: W$^m$ Gorsuch-Times and Ann Dew.

Proved at London 4 April 1794 by Elizabeth the relict. (Holman, 232.)

FRANCIS WYMAN of St. Antholin, London, Callender.

16 Nov. 1789.

Immortal part to the Almighty. Funeral to be carried out at small expense. To M$^r$ Joseph Langhorn 10 guineas. To my wife Mary all the plate, linen, china, books and household goods she brought with her, and such other as she may choose. To son Francis John Wyman all my stock-in-trade, utensils, etc. He to enter into a bond in £1000 to pay my wife £30 yearly for her life out of my freehold messuage in Queen Street in S$^t$ Antholin's, with power to make entry and distrain in case of non-payment. My wife, said son and Joseph Langhorn to be executors.

Witnesses: James Collins, Wm. Pagelia's clerk, Wm. Moore.

*Codicil.* 16 June 1792. My wife to have the use of my messuage and furniture at Queen Street for 6 months after my death.

Witnesses: W^m Allemond, Samuel Green.

Proved at London 2 Nov. 1792 by the executors named. (Fountain, 587.)

JOSEPH WENMAN of Fleet Street, London, Bookseller and Stationer.

2 March 1790.

To Henry Ball, senior, and George Kearsley, senior, five guineas for rings. My messuages in Crown Court to wife Elizabeth. To the said Elizabeth, Richard Baker of Leadenhall Street, haberdasher, and George Bowen of Ludgate Hill, perfumer, all stock-in-trade, books, debts, etc., etc., to carry on the trade, to raise £800 new 4 per cent. Bank annuities, and to apprentice my sons Joseph and Richard Henry. My wife to take son Joseph as her apprentice, and at the age of 25 admit him as partner in the business. To my executors I leave £800 stock for the use of my children Elizabeth, Joseph, Richard Henry and Charlotte for their education, etc. To my wife all household furniture, linen, china, wearing-apparel and pictures.

Witnesses: James Laverlade, Joseph Littler, J. H. Fox, Bride Lane.

Proved at London 13 March 1790 by the executors named. (Bishop, 165.)

ANN WENMAN of Windsor, co. Berks, daughter of Mary Walker, widow.

11 April 1791.

Funeral expenses and debts to be paid. I desire to be buried in the cloister of the Collegiate Church of Windsor near my mother. To [blank] daughter of Samuel and Elizabeth Hunt of Heathfield, Sussex, £200 New South Sea Annuities. To the minister of Heathfield for the time being the like, the interest to be paid to four poor widows being householders. The like sum to Isaac, Mark and Neill Johnson, my trustees, for their trouble. To Mr. Charles Wenman, my husband, £200. All household goods to

Richard Hook of Heathfield, except a set of china, which I leave to my friend M^rs Richardson, daughter of Neill Johnson. To the children of the late Joseph Harmer of Heathfield £150, and the residue among the children of Jonathan Harmer his brother. Executors: Isaac Mark and Neill Johnson.

Witnesses: David Rees, J. Richardson.

12 Jan. 1820. Administration granted with limitations to Jonathan, son of Jonathan Harmer, one of the residuary legatees, and finally on 19 June 1821, he being next of kin. (Kent, 52.)

The Rev. RICHARD WAINMAN, clerk, B.C.L., Rector of Bodington, Northants.

1 Dec. 1791.

To be buried in the chancel at Bodington. To my cousin William Bagnold of Halifax, Yk., all my closes, etc., in Bodington, in White Land Field, to sell the same to my successor in preference to any other, to pay debts and funeral expenses. To my nephews Richard Bradley Wainman and William Wainman and my nieces Elizabeth, Mary Ann and Caroline Wainman, children of my brother William Wainman, Esq., £10 each. To the wife of the Rev^d D^r Bates £50. To Miss Sally, daughter of my second cousin Joseph Edwards, Esq., £50. To servant Sarah Howorth £40 and Samuel Brown the like, if they be not living with me at my death, to pass to the churchwardens. To William Willes, William Weston, William Walton and John Withabed, inhabitants of Bodington, £100 in trust, the interest to be divided among 5 poor persons of the parish at the discretion of the Rector. The residue to be spent to educate poor children of the parish. Sole executor William Bagnold.

Witnesses: Thomas Budd, William Bassett, John Leigh.

Proved at London 19 Feb. 1808 by William Bagnold. (Ely, 160.)

The Honble. THOMAS FRANCIS WENMAN.

29 Dec. 1793.

To be buried where I may hap to die, but if I die at Oxford, within the Chapel of All Souls' College. To Lord

Wenman £100. To Richard Wenman £20. To nephew William Wykeham £20. To niece Harriet Wykeham £20. To John Edmunds, grocer, my servant, £500. To Frederick his son, £100. To All Souls' College £100. To the servant with me at my death, my wearing apparel. To the Rev[d] Edward Williams of Leighton, Salop, all my books, chemical apparatus, preparations, dried plants and all my natural curiosities, with the cases and drawers containing them. Residue to my nephew Philip Wykeham of Oriel College. Brother Lord Wenman to be executor.

The handwriting of the will sworn to by John Hollier of Thame, and John Dunn of Thame Park, 20 April 1796.

Proved at London 26 April 1796 by Philip, Viscount Wenman. (Harris, 230.)

The Hon. RICHARD WENMAN of Bristol, Esquire.
20 Dec. 1794.

Debts and funeral expenses to be paid. To Alice Hull, my housekeeper, my freehold messuage bought of Anthony Palmer Collings, Esq., in Park Street, Bristol, wherein I dwell, and all money, securities, jewels, watches, post chaise, books, plate, pictures, linen, etc. She to pay the Rev[d] John Cauldfields, eldest son of William [blank] now in Ireland, £100. To the godson of my late wife Jannet Wenman £100. To Miss Cecilia Forest £100. To Samuel West my servant £10 and my wearing linen and apparel. To my servant Kitty Philpott five guineas, all my servants to have decent mourning. I desire to be interred in Clifton Church. Executrix Alice Hull.

Witnesses: James and Mathew Windey and H. C. Windey.

*Codicil*, 20 Dec. 1794. To Samuel West £50 in lieu of the £10 previously left to him. Witnesses as above.

Proved at London 22 Oct. 1799 by Alice Hull, executrix. (Howe, 753.)

SARAH WYMENT of Daventry, Northants, Spinster.
2 April 1795.

To my sister Catherine Harrison all my freehold estates in Cleydon, co. Oxon, my wearing apparel, and the Bible and Prayerbook given my mother by the Rev. Jas. Asslock. Residue of books between nephew Samuel Montgomery and niece Catherine Harrison. To said niece my house in Daventry bought of Samuel Castoll, my plate, linen, china, etc., and to her seven children £100 each. To my nephew Samuel Montgomery £300, and on the receipt is to give a bond to pay neice Catherine £8 yearly, and deliver her the goods which were my sister Elizabeth's. To cousin Mary Clarke of Rugby four guineas yearly. All monies, mortgages, etc., in public funds to sister Catherine and Titus Wadsworth of Daventry, gent., to pay my debts and funeral charges. The said Catherine and Titus to be executors.

Witnesses: Ann Edwards, Martha Shaw and James Shaw.

*Codicil*, 24 March 1801. Since my brother-in-law and his daughter Sarah are dead, and his son Henry Bradshaw Harrison, Rector of Bugbrook, has possessed himself of estates intended for other children, I revoke his legacy of £100, and give all those given to my brother-in-law and niece Sarah to the other 5 children Catherine, Elizabeth, Samuel Wyment, William Bagshaw, and Lewis.

Witnesses: Ann and Mary Edwards and Martha Shaw.

Proved at London 21 Oct. 1802 by Catherine and Titus the Executors. (Kenyon, 790.)

ELIZABETH WYMAN of Stonebury in Little Hormead, co. Herts, widow.

18 Aug. 1795.

Soul to God. To my daughter Fanny Wayman my best bedstead with the yellow morine furniture and bedding. To my daughter Katherine nine guineas in lieu of a bedstead, my best goose feather bed, etc. To my daughters Fanny and Katherine Wyman, Rose Sworder and Elizabeth Chapman, all the rest of my furniture and plate, linen, etc. To my sons William, Richard, Francis and George Wyman £200 each. Son-in-law William Sworder of Ansey Bury, co. Herts, farmer, and John Chapman of Hormead Hall, farmer, my executors, such money as will raise an annuity of £10 to be paid Maria Calvert for life, pursuant to the will of

Mr. Edward Faircloth my brother-in-law, and after to the use of my four daughters. To my Executors I give my farm and lands in Stansted Mountfitchett, co. Essex, in the occupation of Joseph Ryder upon trust to pay the profits to my daughter Katherine for life, with remainder to the heirs of my body. To my daughters Fanny Rose and Elizabeth £900 each, and the interest of £300 to Katherine. Residue of personal estate to be divided between my daughters.

Witnesses: John Neild, Martha Pullett and Thomas Nicholson.

Proved at London 21 May 1798 by Messrs. Sworder and Chapman. (Walpole, 373.)

THOMAS WAINMAN of Populwick, co. Notts, gentleman.

28 Dec. 1797.

To my friends Robert Sykes of Nottingham, draper, and John Langley of Popplewick, schoolmaster, £1000 3 per cent. Bank Annuities, in trust to pay my sister Sarah Wainman and niece Theodosia Wainman, or the survivor for life. After their decease to sell the said securities, and reinvest for the benefit of the issue of my cousins John Wainman and Jane Oliver and the issue of my niece Elizabeth Meares. Residue to said trustees in trust to pay my wife an annuity for life, and upon her decease to the children of my abovesaid cousins. Residue to wife.

Witnesses: Charles Betney, Samuel Bolton.

Proved at London 7 May 1798 by John Langley and Robert Sykes, executors. (Walpole, 370.)

PHILIP LORD WENMAN, VISCOUNT TUAM.

15 Feb. 1798.

To be buried at Witney, privately and not expensively. All freehold estate at Twyford, Bucks, and Charndon and elsewhere in Great Britain, to Richard Clerke of Kingston in Aston Rowant, Oxon, and Philip Wroughton Clerke of Shavington, Bucks, in trust to sell the said estate and pay off the mortgage thereon, my debts and funeral expenses,

and to further pay to nephew William Richard Wykham
£100 for mourning. To my neice Harriett Mary Bertie
£100. To my uncle The Hon^{ble} Richard Wenman £100.
To my aunt Ann Herbert £100. To serv^t Richard Dunn
£20 annually, Mary Davis, waiting woman to my wife Lady
Eleanor, £30 yearly. Residue to nephew Philip Thomas
Wykham of All Souls' College, Oxford. To my wife
all jewels, trinkets, seals and watches, pictures, prints,
drawings, books, etc., in her bed-chamber and dressing-
room at Thame Park, and £400, also the plate, furniture
and painted glass in my chapel at Thame. To Miss
Joice and Miss Louisa Gallin 50 guineas each for
mourning. To my Bailif Izard Wildegoose £50. To the
poor of Thame £20, of Sydenham £15, of Witney £20, of
Twyford £20, of Kingsey £15. Residue to nephew Philip
Thomas Wykham. He and my two Trustees to be
executors.

Witnesses: Henry Dimmock, John Jaques, William
Eeles of Thame.

*Codicil*, 3 Jan. 1799. Desiring to be buried at Thame.

Proved in London 28 April 1800 by Richard Clerke,
Esq., and Philip Tho. Wykham. (Adderley, 331.)


OGLETHORPE WAINMAN of Wisbech in the Isle of Ely,
Doctor of Physic.

23 April 1799.

Debts to be paid. To my sister Eleanor Wainman
£20 annually for life, and a messuage and lands at
Wickenstill near Coline, co. Lanc., late my father's.
Wife Ann and friends William Wainman of Carliea, co.
York, Esq., and Thomas Pulvatoft of Spalding, co. Linc.,
Esq., To hold said messuage, buildings and lands in
Wickerstill in trust for the benefit of my wife and
children until daughter Marian come of age, when she
is to receive a third part. Another share to daughter
Julia Beatrix when 21, the remaining part to wife. To
servant Ann Edgson £5 yearly for life. Residue to wife.

Witnesses: Ann Polton, Thomas Rands, Robert
Barker.

Proved at London 30 June 1800 by Ann and Thomas.
(Adderley, 497.)

F

WILLIAM WAINMAN, late of Chislehurst, co. Kent, gardener,
and of Buttercrombe, co. York, gent.
14 Nov. 1800.

To Hannah, daughter of Thomas Tiplady of Buttercrombe, yeoman, my goddaughter, £20. To John Brigham of the same, yeoman, and Sarah his wife, £10. To the two daughters of William Brigham, yeoman, £10 each, wearing apparel and linen to the said William. £200 owing me upon bond by John Making, gent., and Richard Darley of Alsby Park, gent., to John Brigham the younger and William Brigham in trust, to pay the interest to my sister Elizabeth, widow of William Ruddall of Buttercrombe, yeoman, with remainder to her children, one of whom, Thomas, is not capable of receiving his share, which must remain in trust. The £200 secured on mortgage to Joseph Lovearing of Dorset Street, Spital Fields, London, Carpenter, I place with the said trustees to pay the interest to my sister Jane, widow of Enoch Radge of Dunington, Yk., yeoman, with remainder to her children. Residue to John and William Brigham and their children.

Witnesses: W. Holmes of Stildegate, yeoman, Mathew Holmes of the same, currier, Michael Ellis, gent.

Proved before the Commissary of the Archbishop of York 7 Feb. 1806, and in London 17 Feb. 1806 by John and William Brigham. (Pitt, 179.)

ELEANOR, VISCOUNTESS WENMAN.
25 April 1803.

To my nephew Thomas Stapleton of the Grove at Richmond, Yk., son of my sister Lady Mary Stapleton, all my real and personal property, he to be executor.

Witnesses: Job Thomas Bennett, Jessey and Louisa Gallini.

Proved at London 24 April 1804 by Thomas. (Heseltine, 299.)

HENRICH WEIMAN *alias* WEYMAN *alias* HENRICH WEIMAN
of White Cross Street, Middlesex, Sugar baker.
23 Sept. 1803.

To each of my sisters and brothers 10 rix dollars for mourning. To John and Dorothea, son and daughter of my sister Ahloiton, 5 shillings each for mourning. To Henrich, son of my sister Geston, the like, residue to father and mother.

Witnesses: Claus Pulchester, Lois Ann Rosterharun, Johan Fickon.

Copied from the English, attested by Christian Focke. Bremen, 31 Jan. 1818. Notarial attestation by D. Migail and Bach, D.N.P.

Admon. granted 23 Sept. 1815 to Henrich the father. (Pakenham, 522.)

MANSELL WAYMAN of St. Paul's, Deptford, Shipwright.

25 Nov. 1808.

All effects to wife Rebecca, on her death to my daughters Rebecca Bradley, Hannah Wayman and Harriot Patten in equal shares. Executors: Wife and Michael Dixon, shipwright.

Witnesses: W<sup>m</sup> Maccraw and W<sup>m</sup> Boyd.

Proved at London 5 July 1810 by the said executors. (Collingwood, 398.)

EDWARD WHYMAN of Longthorpe in the Liberty of Peterborough and County of Northampton.

3 May 1813.

All effects to wife Catherine, whom I appoint Executrix.
Witnesses: William Bailey, John Hook.
Proved at London 10 Nov. 1813 by the said Catherine (Heathfield, 573.)

## ADMINISTRATIONS.

Wymond, Dorothy, of Rye, co. Sussex, widow, 4 Sept. 1560, to William her son.     1560, f. 18.

Wymonde, William, of Biddenden, co. Kent, 31 Aug. 1565, to John his brother.     1565, f. 96.

Wymonde, Johanna, of the same, to the like.     1565, f. 96.

Wenman, Thomas, of Witney Park, co. Oxon, 4 May 1582, to Jane, relict, and John, son, of deceased.
    1581—3, f. 37.

Wayman, Francis, of Bristol, 13 May 1584, to Elizabeth Wayman alias Cooke, his sister.     1583—6, f. 172.

Wayman, Robert, of St. Olave, Southwark, co. Surrey, 27 Jan. 1592, to Lucy his widow.     1592, f. 2.

Weyman, Francis, of Bristol, 26 Aug. 1592, to Juliana Wayman alias Horte, his mother.     1592, f. 27.

Wayman, Diricus, of London, 3 April 1595, to Anne, widow of Thomas Rutlande of Cavendish, co. Suffolk.
    1595, f. 130.

Wymond, John, of Llanteglas, co. Cornwall, 30 Jan. 1600, to Joane his relict.     1600, f. 37.

Waineman, Sir Ferdinand, Knight, of Bretts in Aveley co. Essex, to Frances his relict, 5 Feb. 1611.
    1611, f. 5.

Wymant, Andrew, of St. Olave's, Southwark, co. Surrey, 16 Jan. 1612, to Martha his widow.     1612, f. 45.

Wyman, William, of St. Nicholas, Gloucester, 26 March 1616, to Edward Symons, feltmaker of that city, pending settlement of the suit between him and Eleanor Holder, widow.     1619, f. 109.

Wenman alias Berniger, Margery, of St. Gregory's [by St. Paul's], London, 9 Nov. 1619, to Henry, her

## ADMINISTRATIONS.

husband, pending the minority of Richard Wenman, her son. 1619, f. 42.

Weymond, Edwards, *in partibus*, 25 June 1627, to Edward Troute, a creditor. 1627, f. 157.

Wayneman, Humphrey, of Bercott in Buckland, co. Berks, 23 March 1634, to James Gresham of East Greenwich, co. Kent, gent. 1634-5, f. 87.

Wymond, Thomas, of Lainvot, co. Cornwall, widower, 25 Sept. 1630, to John his son. 1630, Sept., f. 190.

Wenman, Richard, of Sowlederne, co. Oxon, 11 Sept. 1637, to Thomas his son. 1636—8, f. 110.

Wayneman, Humphrey, of London, 25 June 1641, to Sarah his relict. 1641, f. 46.

Wainman alias Ormerod, Sarah Ormerod alias Wainman of Heythrop, co. Oxon, 1650, to Peter Ormerod her husband. 1650, f. 5.

Wainman, Thomas, of Dedington, co. Oxon, 8 July 1650, to Peter Ormerod, clerk. 1650, f. 120.

Wainman, Anthony, *in partibus*, 8 July 1650, to Peter Ormerod, clerk. 1650, f. 120.

Weyman, Morris, *in partibus*, 18 August 1651, to John Weyman his brother 1650, f. 137.

Waineman, William, late of Embsey, co. York, widower, 27 Sept. 1651, to Thomas his son. 1650, f. 152.

Waineman, Henry, late of Ugthorpe, co. York, 11 June 1655, to Mary, relict of deceased. 1655, f. 120.

Weyman, Thomas, of "the Swiftsure," 29 Sept. 1655, to Pethia his sister. 1655, f. 180.

Wayneman, William, of York, 3 Jan. 1657, to Christopher his only son 1657, f. 7.

Chippendale alias Wayneman, Margaret, of York, 22 June 1657, to William Waineman her brother. 1657, f. 136.

**Wayman, Robert, of Rington in Great Canford, co. Dorset, 22 May 1658, to Katherine his relict.** 1658, f. 114.

Wyman, John, of Wellingborough, co. Northants, 1 Dec. 1658, to Mary his relict. 1658, f. 271.

Weyman, Walter, *in partibus*, on H.M.S. "Le Fairfax," 20 Nov. 1673, to Isaaca his sister, wife of Richard Fuchett.

Wayman, Robert, of St. Olave, Southwark, 15 Jan. 1679-80, to George Taylor, next-of-kin. 1680, Jan.

Waiman, Richard, of Deptford, on board the SS. "Le Ashia," 15 June 1680, to Richard his father.
1680, Jan.

Wayman, Richard, *in partibus*, on "Le Devonshire" and after on "Le Assistance," of Berwick, 14 July 1693, to Mary, wife of Richard Bennet, proxy of Catherine, widow of deceased. 1693, July.

Whayman, Thomas, *in partibus*, of St. Mary, Whitechapel, on board "Le Lyon," 1 Dec. 1693, to Thomas Ting, creditor.

Wayman, John, *in partibus*, of H.M.S. "Le Warwick." 28 March 1698, to Robert Bowden, creditor.
1698, March.

Wainman, Joseph, *in partibus*, 19 Sept. 1698, to Ann Davison, proxy of Isabel his relict, living at Bloxham.
1698, Sept.

Wenman, Richard, of St. Michael, Cornhill, London, 8 Oct. 1698, to Martha his widow. 1698, Oct.

Wenman, William, of St. Giles-in-the-Fields, Middlesex, 24 Aug. 1708, to Anne his relict. 1708, f. 157.

Wanman alias Wayman, George, of the ship "Le Deal Castle," 8 Aug. 1711, to Thomas Jackson, next-of-kin.
1711, f. 143.

Wayman, Samuel, of H.M.S. "Swiftsure," 11 Dec. 1711, to George Turill, creditor. 1711, f. 237.

Weyman, Judith, of East Greenwich, co. Kent, 9 Sept. 1718, to Sarah her daughter, wife of Charles Branck.
1718, Sept.

Wyman alias Wayman, Edward, of Northampton, 15 Aug. 1722, to Thomas Church, creditor, Eliza Easton, Thomas Wayman and Mary Wayman, his children, renouncing. 1722, Aug.

Weyman, Judith, of St. Saviour, Southwark, 30 Sept. 1727, to Jacob her son. 1727, Sept.

Wenman, Lord, January 1730. Calendar only.

Wenman, Richard, of St. George's, Hanover Square, at Brussels with the Royal Horse Guards Blue, 5 May 1744, to Mathew Lamb, Esq., creditor, William Wenman and George his brother, Frances Coltrel his niece, William and Charlotte Coltrel and Charles their father renouncing. 1744, May.

Wainman, William, of Robin Hood's Bay, York, on board H.M.S. "The Royal Sovereign," 26 June 1744, to George Jackson, attorney of Elizabeth Wenman the widow. 1744, June.

Wayman, Thomas, Surgeon's Mate on H.M.S. "Duke," to Lewis Wayman his father, 17 June 1751.
1751, June.

Waymon, Isabella, of St. Botolph's, Aldgate, London, widow, 5 Feb. 1754, to John her son. 1754, Feb.

Wyman, Mary, of St. Mary's, Whitechapel, co. Mdx., 21 Jan. 1758, to Elizabeth Wyman her daughter.
1758, Jan.

Wayman, William, seaman on H.M.S. "Sunderland," 5 May 1762, to William Wayman his father.
1762, May.

Wainman, William, of St. Margaret's, Westminster, 7 Sept. 1762, to Elizabeth Wainman the widow.
1762, Sept.

Wayman, William, of Ramsey, co. Essex, 30 Dec. 1763, to Thomas Cooper, creditor, Power Wayman the widow renouncing. 1763, Dec.

## ADMINISTRATIONS.

Wayman, Lewis, of **Kimbolton**, Hunts, 22 July 1764, to Susanna, widow of deceased. 1764, July.

Wayman, John Godfrey, of St. Nicolas, Rochester, on H.M.S. "Dreadnought," 15 Aug. 1766, to Mary Wayman his widow. 1766, Aug.

Bunyon, Martha, née Wenman, Martha, of St. George's, Bloomsbury, 5 May 1770, to James Bunyon her husband. 1770, May.

Wayman, John, of St. Mildred in the Poultry, 4 Dec. 1770, to Thomas Price, creditor, Mary the widow renouncing for herself and Frederick her son.
1770, Dec.

Wayman, John, of St. Mary Magdalene, Bermondsey, co. Surrey, 29 July 1772, to Mary, relict of deceased.
1772, July.

Wayman, John Michael, alias Weyman, of St. Mary's, Islington, co. Mdx., and of Eltham, co. Kent, bachelor, 23 Sept. 1774, to George his brother. 1774, Sept.

Wenman, Thomas, of St. Saviour's, Southwark, co. Surrey, 30 Aug. 1775, to Sarah Wenman, widow, mother of deceased. 1775, Aug.

Wayman, Susannah, of Weymouth, co. Dorset, widow, 19 May 1780, to Isaac her son. 1780, May.

Whayman, William, of St. Andrew's, Holborne, co. Mdx., 6 Aug. 1782, to Oliver, wife of Richard Perkins, relict of deceased. 1782, Aug.

Wayman, Robert, of St. Olave's, Southwark, on the High Seas, 17 Jan. 1780, to George Taylor, next of kin.
1780, Jan.

Wainman, Elizabeth, of Balne, co. Yk., 12 Nov. 1789, to John her husband. 1789, Nov.

Wayman, John, of St. Mary's, Whitechapel, 24 April 1795, to Ann his relict. 1795, April.

Waymand, Daniel, of H.M.S. "Centaur," bachelor, 23 Sept. 1796, to John his father. 1796, Sept.

## ADMINISTRATIONS. 73

Wayman, Hannah, widow, of Guy's Hospital, Southwark, 28 May 1801, to William Petford her brother.
1801, May.

Wayman, Daniel, of St. Mary's, Whitechapel, 11 July 1801, to Cassiah his widow. 1801, July.

Wyman, James, of Blackmore Street, Clare Market in St. Clement Danes, London, widower, 12 Sept. 1801, to Anne, wife of Nathaniel Birch, his daughter.
1801, Sept.

Wenman, Janet, formerly of Corfield, widow, 26 Sept. 1801, late of Bristol Hot Wells, to James Campbell, Esq., her cousin german, the Honble. Richard Wenman her husband dying without administering.
1801, Sept.

Wayman, William, 13 July 1801, of H.M.S. "Resistance," to Cassiah his relict. 1801, July.

Wayman, Elizabeth, of Hatch in Northill, co. Beds, widow, to William Wayman her son, 9 Dec. 1802.
1802, Dec.

Weyman, William, of H.M.S. "Abergavenny," bachelor, 3 Dec. 1802, to Mary, wife of Manning Humber, his mother. 1802, Dec.

Wyman, Joseph, of Eyre Street Hill in St. Andrew's, Holborn, and Great Warner Street in St. James', Clerkenwell, 30 Dec. 1807, to Sarah the widow.

Weymond, John, alias Hagger, of H.M.S. "Primrose" and H.M.S. "Mediator," 31 July 1809, to Thomas Hagger his father. 1809, July.

Wyman, Thomas, of Wades Mill in Standon, co. Herts, to Sarah his widow, 17 Oct. 1810. 1810, Oct.

Weyman, Thomas, of St. Michael's, Dublin, Sergeant, 69th Regiment of Foot in the East Indies, 10 Oct. 1815, to Catherine his widow. 1815, Oct.

Wenman, Charles, of New Windsor, co. Berks, and late

of Henley, co. Oxon, widower, 30 March 1816, to Benjamin Taylor his cousin german. 1816, March.

Hannam alias Wainman, Denby, of H.M.S. "Captain Belleisle" and Dominica, bachelor, 29 Oct. 1817, to John his brother. 1817, Oct.

Wenman, Ann, June 21. "Special administration of the rest of the goods entered at length." [This entry apparently never completed.] 1821, June.

Wayman, Rebecca, late of Deptford, co. Kent, widow, 2 June 1821, to Rebecca, wife of John Badley, her daughter. 1821, June.

# GLOSSARY.

*Arrass.* The better kind of tapestry extended on screens and used as a wall decoration.
*Banner cloth.* The embroidered or painted pendant suspended from a cross pole.
*Bogye.* Lambskin or Budge dressed with the wool outwards.
*Brennyng.* Burning.
*Broad gold.* Old and thin rials or angels; coins of James I. and Charles I.
*Calabre.* A kind of fur obtained from some foreign squirrel.
*Calendar.* For calenderer, one who calenders cloth.
*Carsey.* A form of kersey, a coarse woollen fabric.
*Celour and testour.* The canopy over a bedstead, either supported by a frame or suspended from the ceiling.
*Chamlet.* A beautiful Eastern fabric of camel's hair mixed with silk.
*Cope.* The embroidered cloak used as the principal vestment in choir.
*Dirge.* Matins for the dead. A word derived from the Antiphon *Dirige gressos meos.* Sung at Matins on the morning of the burial. (Ps. v. 8.) Direct, O Lord my God, my way in Thy sight.
*Duckett, ducat.* A gold coin used in most countries of Europe, worth about 9s. 4d. The silver ducat used in Italy was worth 3s. 6d. This was first issued by Roger II. of Sicily in 1140.
*Dymescent.* A girdle. The front of gold or silver work; the hinder part of silk.
*Figury.* Ornamented with designs or patterns.
*Fryse.* A coarse woollen fabric with a nap.
*Fur Olyaunce.* A kind of fur named after the city of Orleans.
*Gennew, ginnell.* A finger-ring constructed to form two.
*Jerkin.* A doublet.

# GLOSSARY.

*Kirtle.* A woman's gown, usually an outer petticoat.
*Lowe work.* Chased work in low relief.
*Masser (Mazer).* A bowl of maple or other wood rimmed with silver or formed of precious metal.
*Mayden heads.* Spoons in which the head of the Blessed Virgin Mary replaced the earlier knob handle.
*Mesolin (Maslin).* Mixed grain, *i.e.*, rye and wheat.
*Murrey.* Mulberry colour.
*Mynks.* Fur of the mink-otter.
*Naperye.* Table linen.
*Pall or Canapie.* The lace or embroidered cover for the hanging pyx containing the Blessed Sacrament or Host.
*Pewke.* Puce colour.
*Placebo.* Vespers for the dead, so named from the Antiphon.
*Pomander.* A perfume ball commonly suspended at the girdle.
*Prik-song.* Music noted or pricked. Not sung from memory.
*Purfelde.* Ornamented with trimming, usually a border of embroidery, lace or fur.
*P' of Spark.* A pair of diamonds.
*Salve.* The Ave Maria or Angelic Salutation.
*Sarsenet.* A fine and soft silk material.
*Shanks.* Fur from the leg of an animal.
*Stole werke.* Embroidered in strips.
*Tabernacle.* A niche for a statue.
*Tawney.* Orange colour.
*Tobine Jerkin.* One embroidered in strips with gold thread and colours.
*Torch.* A large wax candle carried in the hand.

( 77 )

# GENERAL INDEX.

## A

Abbots Barton, Glouc., 24.
Abbott, Tho., 22.
Abington, Berks, 11.
  Almshouse, 2.
  Church, 2.
  Lord, 54.
Acres, Jn., 30.
Adams, Jn., 6.
Ades, Barb., 17 ; Jn., 17.
Ahloiton, Dor., 67 ; Jn., 67.
Alford, Sar., 54.
Allemond, Wm., 60.
Allesley, War., 27.
Allworthy, Ann, 55.
Almont, Jas., 30.
Alsby Park, 66.
Altar Cloth, 7.
  Cross, 7.
  Table, 8.
Amon, Cath., 22.
Amy, Prioress of St. Lawr., 8.
Anderton, Sar., 50.
Angworth, Ric., 20.
Ansey Bury, Herts, 63.
Armour, 20.
Arms of Thurston, 7-8.
Arras, 7.
Arters, Ann, 21 ; Ric., 21.
Asslock, Rev. Jas., 63.
Aston Rowant, Oxon, 26, 64.
Atkytson, Hy., 16.
Austin, Eliz., 50.
Aveley, Essex, 68.
Awcock, Wm., 17.
Ayraye, Edw., 20.

## B

Bacon, Fra., 29 ; Tho., 29.
Badley, Jn., 74 ; Rebecca, 74.
Bagnold. Wm., 61.
Bailey, Wm., 67.
Baker, Jn., 19 ; Ric., 60 ; Tho., 54 ; Wm., 24.
Bakwell, Ric., 31.
Ball, Hy., 60.
Balle, Eliz., 27.
Balne, York, 72.
Bambrooke, Hy., 17.
Barett, Jn., 9.
Barker, Rob., 65.
Barnes, Jn., 26.
Barrett, Tho., 2, 9, 10.
Barry, Vinc., 27, 31.
Barton, Ma. B., 24.
Bassett, Wm., 61.
Bates, Dr., 61.
Batt, Miss, 52.
Baxster, Joane, 6 ; Jn., 6 ; Mgt., 6 ; Ric., 10.
Baylye, Tho., 17.
Baynam. Dor., 27.
Beard, Hy., 25.
Bedford, 16.
Bedson, Salop, 50.
Beerley, Ric., 30.
Belchamber, Jn., 29.
Bellamour, Eliz., 53.
Bells, repair of, 2, 11.
  ringing, 1.
Benet, Sir Jn., 20.
Benguyn, Jn., 17.
Benhey, Oxon, 2.
Bennet, Ma., 70 ; Ric., 70.
Bennett, Job Tho., 66.
Benson, Rob., 14.
Bercot, Berks, 69.
Bergo, Abrah., 30 ; Sar., 30.
Berkyng Chapel, 6.
Bermondsey, 72.
Berniger, Mgy., 68.
Bertie, Harrt. M., 65.
Berwick, 70.
Best, Jn., 15.
Bethlehem Hospital, 7.
Bethnal Green, 8, 52.
Betney, Chas., 64.
Bevin, Jn., 28.
Biddenden. Kent, 68.
Binckens, Jn., 15.
Birch, Anne, 73 ; Nath., 73.
Birchett, Tho., 15.
Birmingham, 23, 30, 49.
  Leays Lane, 30.

Birmingham—*continued.*
  Priors Conygree, 30.
  St. Mary, 57.
  Walmore Lane, 30.
Bishop, Jas., 53 ; Sarah, 53.
Blackwell, Ric., 16.
Blair, Jas., 49.
Blewbury, Berks. 2.
Bloxham, Oxon, 70.
Bodington. Nthts., 61.
Bolton, Sam., 64.
Book, Joane, 9.
Boram, Jn., 26.
Botting, Jn., 22.
Bouchery, Sar., 31.
Bowden. Rob., 70.
Bowen, Geo., 60.
Boyd, Wm., 67.
Bradley, Rebecca, 67.
Bradwell, Oxon, 2.
Bramble, Susa., 24.
Branck, Chas., 70 ; Sar., 70.
Braughing, 59.
Bray, Berks, 50.
Bremen, 67.
Brent, Edw., 27.
Brickell, Jn., 20.
Briggs, Aug., 29.
Brigham, Jn., 66 ; Sar., 66 ; Wm., 66.
Brings, 9.
Bristol, 68.
  Hot Wells, 73.
  Park St., 62.
Broke. Mr., 9.
Bromfields, Giles, 13.
Bromley, 59.
Brooke, Jn., 28 ; Tho., 18, 32.
Brookethorpe, Glouc., 22-3.
Brougham, Thos., 49.
Broughton, Jn., 18.
Browderas, Mort., 9.
Browne, Edw., 22 ; Eliz., 9 ; Jas., 22 ; Jn., 9, 10 ; Ma., 22 ; Sam., 61 ; Sar., 22 ; Sus., 22.
Brudenell, Edm., 16.
Brussels, 71.
Buchanan, Ma., 57.
Buckland, Berks, 69.
Budd, Tho., 61.
Bugbrook, Northts., 63.
Bully, Wm., 9.
Bulton, Agn., 17 ; Joan, 17 ; Jn., 17.
Bunne, Jn., 17.
Bunyon, Jas., 72 ; Martha, 72.
Burgess, Ric., 17.
Burton, Jn., 9.
Busbye, Eliz., 17.
Butler, Ma., 56 ; Tho., 9.

Buttercrombe, York, 66.
Buxsted, Sussex, 17.
Byddell, Agn., 13.
Byrd, Joan, 9.
Byver, Jas., 10.

C

Cadman, Wm., 18.
Calard. Eliz., 9 ; Ric., 9.
Calfield, Geo., 18.
Calvert, Ma., 63.
Cambridge Univ., 7.
Cammell, Eliz., 27.
Campbell, Jas., 73.
Canner, 28.
Canopy, 2.
Canterbury, St. Aug., 8.
  St. Lawr., 8.
Capps, Edw., 31.
Carliea, York, 65.
Carlisle, C. of, 25.
Caroles. Ric., 23.
Carswell, Oxon, 12, 25, 29.
Carter, Bern., 19 ; Geo., 27.
Castell, Mgt., 9 ; Sam., 63.
Cauldfields, Jn., 62 ; Wm., 62.
Caunton, Eliz., 8 ; Jn., 8, 9 ; Maud, 8, 9 ; Nic., 8.
Cavendish, Suff., 68.
Chadlington, Oxon, 2.
Chapman, Eliz., 59, 63 ; Jn., 59, 63.
Charndon, Oxon, 28, 64.
Chelsea, 25.
Chemson, Ric., 13.
Chichester, 10.
Childers, Mgt., 9.
Chislehurst, Kent, 66.
Christopherson, 9.
Clanfield, Oxon, 2.
Clare Market, Mdx., 73.
Clarke, Eliz., 27 ; Isab., 27 ; Ma., 63 ; Ric., 27 ; Tho., 27.
Clempson, Sir Rog., 14.
Clerke, Fr., 19 ; Ric., 64-5.
Cleydon, Oxon, 62.
Cleysey, Mr., 6.
Clifton, Glouc., 62.
Clun, Salop, 50.
Cobcott, Oxon, 28.
Cock, Ann, 29 ; Eliz., 29 ; Nic., 29.
Coggs, Oxon, 12, 25.
Cogham, Jn., 15.
Coke, Joan, 13 ; Wm., 3.
Colchester, 57.
Colett, 14.
Coline, Lanc., 65.
Colins, Jos., 32.

# GENERAL INDEX.   79

Collier, Ma., 52.
Collings, Anth. P., 62.
Collins, Jas., 59.
Coltrel, Charl., 71 ; Chas., 71 ; Fr., 71.
Coming, Wm., 21.
Conell, 9.
Cook, Ann, 58 ; Eliz., 63 ; Joane. 12-3 ; Jn., 58 ; Ma., 31.
Cookham, Berks, 52.
Cooper, Alice, 50 ; Tho., 71.
Corbet, Ric., 9.
Cordwell, Edm., 19.
Corfield, 73.
Cotten, Walt., 32.
Cottesham, Camb., 26.
Courtney, Ric., 19.
Coveley, Jn., 10.
Creasey, Jn., 52.
Crochington, Ric., 9.
Crosborne, Alex., 17.
Crowe, Ric., 24.
Croydon, Vicar of, 9.
Cubbidge, Phil., 18.
Cublington, Berks, 20.
Culmington, Salop, 50.

## D

Dabber, Edw., 22 ; Joane, 22.
Dacuraye, Tho., 12.
Dakeine, Jn., 26.
Daniel, Cath., 56.
Dannett, 18.
Danvers, Jn., 25.
Darley, Ric., 66.
Daunsey, Jn., 9, 10.
Daventry, Northts., 57, 62.
Davis, Ma., 65.
Davison, Ann, 70 ; Jn., 15.
Dawson, Eliz., 3 ; Jn., 3.
Day, Tho., 58.
Dayken, Rob., 9.
Debenham, Ly., 9.
Dedington, Oxon, 69.
Delve, Ann, 31 ; Jasp., 31 ; Pet., 31.
Denham, Jn., 16.
Deptford, Kent, 53, 70, 74.
Dew, Ann, 59.
Dickens, Wm., 24.
Dimmock, Hy., 65 ; Rob., 17.
Dirge, 1, 11.
Dixon, Mich., 6, 7.
Dobyns, Ric., 21.
Docwra, Tho., 14.
Dollyng, Agn., 8 ; Alice, 8 ; Joan, 8 ; Jn., 8 ; Phil., 8, 9 ; Rog., 8.
Donnington, Sussex, 15.

Dopp, Rog., 17 ; Wm., 17.
Dover, 8.
Dowely, Mrs., 13.
Droke, Jn., 20.
Dublin, St. Michael's, 73.
Duddeston, Staff., 49.
Dudley, Edw., 20.
Dunn, Jn., 62 ; Ric., 65.
Dunverde, Rob., 13.
Duppa, Ric., 50.
Dyer, Anne, 13.
Dyne, Jn., 22 ; Tho., 22.
Dynham, Penel., 28.

## E

Eackly, Jn., 30.
East Greenwich, 70.
Eaton, Sim., 28.
Eden, Sam., 31.
Edgerley, 31.
Edgson, Ann, 65.
Edmunds, Fred., 62 ; Jn., 62.
Edwards, Ann, 63 ; Jos., 61 ; Ma., 63 ; Sally, 61.
Eedes, Wm., 65.
Ellis, Mich., 66.
Eltham, Kent, 72.
Elton, Jn., 14.
Embsey, York, 25, 69.
Ensham, Oxon, 31.
Esher, Surrey, 54, 56.
Eston, Jn., 10, 15.
Eton Coll., 12.
Evenly, Northants, 11.
Exmewe, Eliz., 9 ; Sir Tho., 9 ; Wm., 9.

## F

Facarlye, 14.
Faircloth, Edw., 58, 64.
Fakon, Joan, 8.
Falkland, Visc., 25.
Farnham, Bucks, 50.
Farquarson, 9, 56.
Fellowes, Jon., 32.
Felton, Grace, 54 ; Jn., 9, 54 ; Mgt., 54.
Fenton, Eliz., 3.
Fermor, Emm., 2 ; Joane, 2 ; Jn., 3 ; Lawr., 2 ; Ric., 2, 3 ; Tho., 2 ; Wm., 2, 3.
Fettiplace, Edm., 32.
Fickon, Jn., 67.
Fillongley, War., 27.
Fittes, Eliz., 29 ; Jn., 29.

Flemyngefold, 12.
Floyer, Jn. G., 54.
Focke, Xrist., 67.
Foord, Ja., 25 ; Leon., 25.
Forest, Cecil, 62.
Fortey, Jn., 21.
Foster, Tho., 9.
Fox, J. H., 60.
Fraternity of Clerks, 7.
  Our Lady & St. Tho., 7.
  St. Mary, 1.
  Sixty Priests, 7.
Fraunces, Jn., 14.
Freeman, Jos., 51.
Friars of Oxford, 2.
  of London, 6.
Fringford, Oxon, 16, 17.
Fryser, Tho., 9, 10.
Fuchett, Isaac, 70 ; Ric., 70.
Fytzherbert, Tho., 20.

## G

Gale, Rob., 10 ; Tho., 9.
Gallini, Jesse, 65-6 ; Joice, 65 ; Louisa, 65-6.
Gamadge Hale, Glouc., 19.
Gamage, Eliz., 57.
Gardiners, Dor., 6.
Garratt, Alice, 17.
Gaymer, Rob., 10.
George, Tho., 21.
Gerey, 13.
Gery, Hy., 9.
Geston, 67.
Gifford, Ma., 12 ; Tho., 12.
Gillingham, Kent, 27.
Glasbrooke, Wm., 24.
Glassington, Mr., 20.
Gloucester, Hosp. of St. Jas., 24.
  Barton St., 24.
  Northgate, 24.
  St. Ma. de Lead, 24.
  St. Nic., 68.
Glynne, Wm., 19.
Goffe, Ann, 29 ; Mgt., 28 ; Pet., 29.
Goodenough, Eliz., 52 ; Ma., 52.
Goodhurst, Sussex, 17.
Gorsuch-Times, Wm., 59.
Great Canford, Dorset, 69.
Great John, 9.
Greaves, Ann, 54.
Green, Edw., 56-7 ; Ma., 56 ; Sam., 60 ; Wm., 31.
Greneflat, Wm., 15.
Gresham, Jas., 69.
Guestling, Sussex, 14.
Gybons, 9.
Gyles, Joan, 10.

## H

Hackett, Rog., 18 ; Tho., 24.
Haddon, Edw., 26 ; Ra., 26.
Hagger, Jn., 73 ; Tho., 73.
Haines, Anne, 50 ; Hanh., 49, 50 ; Phœbe, 50 ; Sam., 49.
Halford, Eliz., 25 ; Hugh, 25 ; Jn., 24 ; Steph., 24-5.
Halifax, York, 61.
Hampton Gay, Oxon, 31.
Hannam, Denby, 74.
Hardinge, Hy., 27.
Harefield, Mdx., 23.
Haren, Alice, 16.
Harkins, Geo., 59.
Harmer, Jon., 61 ; Jos., 61.
Harper, Ric., 28.
Harris, Geo., 55.
Harrys, Ric., 23 ; Wm., 20, 24.
Harrison, Cath., 51, 62-3 ; Eliz., 63 ; H. B., 63 ; Jac., 55 ; Joan, 55 ; Lewis, 63 ; Rob., 15 ; Sam., 63 ; Tho., 55 ; Wm. B., 63.
Harscombe, Glouc., 23.
Hatch, Beds, 73.
Hawkes, Anne, 26 ; Joan, 26 ; Ma., 26.
Hawkinge, Cons., 19.
Hawkins, Jn., 57 ; Sar., 27.
Hayley, Berks, 2.
Heathfield, Sussex, 60-1.
Hempstead, Herts, 24.
Henley, Oxon, 74.
Herbert, Ann, 54, 65 ; Jas., 49 ; Soph., 49.
Hergat, Pet. de, 14.
Heritage, Alice, 3.
Hervey, Geo., 49.
Hewins, Alice, 12.
Hewys, Alice, 2 ; Jn., 2.
Heythrop, Oxon, 69.
Hicks, Alice, 50 ; Ann, 50 ; Xpher, 50 ; Eliz., 50 ; Felicia, 50 ; Greg., 50 ; Jas., 50 ; Ma., 50 ; Phœbe, 50 ; Ric., 50 ; Rob., 50 ; Tho., 50 ; Wm., 50.
Higgs, Fra., 13.
Hikman, Eliz., 3.
Hill, Jn., 19.
Hochinson, Jn., 15.
Hodges, Ann, 21.
Holden, Rob., 53.
Holder, Elean., 68.
Holderness, Mr., 9.
Hole, Ann, 23 ; Julian, 23 ; Mgt., 23 ; Martha, 23 ; Rebecca, 23.
Holinburne, a monk, 9.
Holland, E. of, 25.

# GENERAL INDEX. 81

Hollier, Jn., 62.
Holloway. Eliz., 30 ; Sergt., 30.
Holmes, Math., 66 ; W., 66.
Holwell, 12.
Hoo, Wm., 9.
Hoode, Hy., 17 ; Rob., 17.
Hook, Jn., 67 ; Ric., 61 ; Tho., 17.
Hormead, Herts, 58.
  Hall, 63.
Hornsey, Rob., 29.
Horse Guards, 71.
Horte, Julian, 68.
Hosier, Jas., 24.
Hountes, Ric., 18.
Howorth, Sar., 61.
Hoxton, Mdx., 58.
**Hoyge, Mgt., 17.**
**Huddlestone, Sible, 18.**
Hughes, Tho., 28.
**Hull, 56.**
Hull, Alice, 56.
Humber, Ma., 73.
Humfrey, Fab., 12 ; Ric., 12.
Hunt, Eliz., 60 ; Humph., 22 ; Sam., 60.
**Huntington Priory, 11.**
Huntley, Jeptha, 32.
Hutt, Tho., 57.
Hydnam, Beds, 15.
Hynde, Sir Jn., 10.

## I

Icklesham, Sussex, 14.
Ingleton, Jas., 9.
Inn, "Adam and Eve," 53.
Ipswich, 14, 55.
Islington. Mdx., 72.
Iver, Bucks, 32.
Ivychurch, Kent, 14.

## J

Jackson, Geo., 71 ; Judith, 56; Tho., 70.
Jamaica, Port Royal, 31.
James, Jn., 17.
Jaques, Jn., 65.
Jephcott, Tho., 51.
Jerkes, Jas., 29.
Johnson, Neill, 60-1 ; Pet., 51 ; Sar., 51, 52.
Jones, Hy., 32.
**Joyner, Jas., 27.**

## K

Kearsley, Geo., 60.
Kele, Ric., 9.
Kelmscott, Oxon, 2.
Kempson, Hy., 57.
Kennedy, Pet., 55.
Kenward, Jn., 17.
Kervet, Sir Tho., 6.
Kimbolton, Hunts, 72.
King, Tho., 28 ; Wm., 56.
Kingsey, Oxon, 54, 65.
King's Norton, Oxon, 3.
Knight, Wm., 6.
Knightsbridge, Mdx., 20.
Kyrkeby, Jn., 7.
Kyrwyn, Ann, 9.

## L

Lady Mass, 1—7.
Laiman, Wm., 19.
Lainvot, Cornw., 69.
Lamb, Math., 71.
Lambeth (Lamehyth), 1, 10, 12.
Lamkyn, Eliz., 9 ; Jn., 10 ; Tho., 9.
Langdale, Steph., 20.
Langford, Berks, 2.
Langharne, Jn., 18.
Langley, Jn., 64 ; Ma., 32.
Langley Marsh, Bucks, 32, 52.
Langton, Jos., 50.
Languillo, Radn., 50.
Lanhidrock, 18.
Lany, Ric., 6.
Larrens, Ric., 16.
Laurens, Jn., 9, 18.
Laverlade, Jas., 60.
Law, Wm., 30.
Lawe, Anth., 18.
Lawford Hall, Essex, 57.
Lawrence, Ann, 57 ; Wm., 57.
Leach, Jn., 52.
Lee, Kent, 7.
Leedham, Alice, 49.
Leigh, Jn., 61.
Leightborne, Wm., 27.
Leighton, Salop, 62.
Leintwardine, Hereford, 50.
Lewe, 12.
Lewes, Jn., 7.
Lewkenor, Oxon, 28.
Lillie. Edm., 19, 20.
Lincoln Cath., 2, 11, 13.
Littler, Jos., 60.
Llanteglas, Cornwall, 68.
London, 1, 69.
  Aldwich Manor, 54.

G

## GENERAL INDEX.

London—*continued.*
  Blackmore St., 11, 73.
  Bride Lane, 60.
  Bridge, 6.
  Cabinet Court, 57.
  Charterhouse, 7.
  Counters, the, 3.
  Custom of, 3.
  Duke St., 31, 57.
  Eyre St. Hill, 73.
  Fetter Lane, 52.
  Fleet St., 60.
  Friars of, 6.
  Furnival's Inn, 26.
  Goldsmiths' Hall, 7.
  Great Warner St., 73.
  Holborne, 54.
  Honey Lane, 3.
  Jewin St., 53, 58.
  King's Bench Prison, 3.
  King St., 57.
  Lazar Houses of, 7.
  Leadenhall St., 60.
  Lombard St., 1.
  Ludgate Hill, 7, 60.
  Ludgate Prison, 3.
  Marshalsea, the, 3, 7.
  Newgate, 3, 7.
  Nicholas Lane, 58.
  Queen Street, 59.
  St. Alban's, Wood St., 3.
  St. Andrew's, Holb., 26, 72-3.
  St. Antholin, 59.
  St. Bartholomew Exch., 53.
  St. Botolph's, Aldersgate, 15.
  St. Botolph's, Aldgate, 19, 71.
  St. Clement Danes, 73.
  St. Dunstan's W., 27.
  St. Faith's, 23.
  St. Giles's, Cripplegate, 53.
  St. Gregory's, 68.
  St. James's, Clerkenwell, 73.
  St. Magnus, 6, 7, 9.
  St. Martin Vint., 6.
  St. Mary-le-Bone, 55.
  St. Mary Staining, 6.
  St. Mary's, Whitechapel, 72-3.
  St. Mary Woolnoth, 1, 6, 7.
  St. Michael's, Cornhill, 70.
  St. Mildred, Poultry, 72.
  St. Paul's, 7.
  St. Sepulchre's, 16.
  St. Vedast, 6.
  Shoreditch, 22.
  Shotborne Lane, 1.
  Smithfield, 19.
  Spital Fields, 66.
  Strand, the, 14.
  Tower, the, 57.

London—*continued.*
  Vintners' Company, 7.
Longhorn, Jos., 59.
Longthorpe. Northants, 67.
Lovearing, Jos., 66.
Loveday, Tho., 28.
Low, Oxon, 25.
Lowe, Rob., 13.
Lowth, Jn., 9 ; Wm., 9, 10.
Lucy, Wm., 3.
Lyckberry, Edw., 6.
Lydall, Ric., 28, 30.
Lydd, 22.
Lyddel, Fenw., 52.

## M

Mainewen, Cornw., 32.
Making, Jn., 66.
Mark, Isa., 60-1.
Marsh, Jn., 20.
Martindale, Edw., 30.
Martyn, Ja., 28 ; Rbt., 14 ; Tho., 17.
Masham, 9.
Mass of Jesus, 7.
Mathewes, Mgt., 24 ; Rob., 24—26 ; Wm., 24.
May, Mk., 31 ; Tho., 28.
Mazareen, Jn., 53.
Meares, Eliz., 64.
Mede, Joan, 8.
Melborne, Dorset, 3.
Meriden, War., 27.
Metcalfe, Hy., 53.
Meyrick, Edw., 50 ; Joyce, 50.
Michell, Tho., 9.
Mile End, 9.
Miles, Pet., 27.
Milicent, 3.
Miller, Alice, 23 ; Geo., 20 ; Hester, 23.
Milton, Oxon, 11.
Minster Lovell, Oxon, 2.
Moccraw, Wm., 67.
Monox, Mr., 9.
Montgomery, Ma., 51 ; Sam., 63.
Month's Mind, The, 13.
Moore, Eust., 20 ; Jas., 54 ; Wm., 54, 59.
Moreton, Oxon, 28.
Morse, Jas., 21.
Mother Agnes, 6.
Mott, Tho., 59.
Much Hadham, 59.
Munn, Sar., 29.
Mydwynter, Eliz., 13 ; Tho., 13 ; Wm., 13.
Mynott, Jos., 26.

# GENERAL INDEX. 83

## N

Needham, Jn., 52.
Neild, Jn., 64.
Nettleton, Martha, 55.
Newberg, Hy., 57.
Newent, Glouc., 21.
Newland, 12.
Newman, Tho., 12.
New Windsor, 73.
Nicholson, Tho., 64.
Nicolls, Sus., 31.
Norreys, Ly., 18 ; Max, 18 ; Sir Hy.. 18 ; Sir Jn., 18.
Norwich, St. Pet. Manc., 29.
  White Lion St., 29.
Nubery, Ja., 31.

## O

Obit, 1.
Old St., Mdx., 58.
Oley, Wm., 25.
Oliver, Ja., 64.
Oneley, Jn., 51.
Organ, Tho., 23.
Ormerod, Pet., 69 ; Sar., 69.
Ormskirk, Lanc., 52.
Orton, Jn., 31.
Osborne, Jn., 10.
Owens, Evan, 58.
Oxford, 2.
  All Souls Coll., 61, 65.
  Castle, 11.
  Friars of, 11.
  Lincoln Coll., 31.
  Oriel Coll., 62.
  Univ., 7.

## P

Pagelia, Wm., 59.
Painter, Alk., 27.
Pall, 2.
Palmer, 9 ; Jasp., 15.
Parkes, Tho. D., 52.
Parkinson, Hy., 55.
Parnel, 9.
Parsons. Edw., 57 ; Eliz., 57.
Patten, Harrt., 67.
Pauncefote, Grimb., 21.
Payne, Sus., 17 ; Walt., 30.
Pedred, Wm., 14.
Pemberton, Hugh, 1 ; Ric., 14.
Pembroke, E. of, 49.
Penny, Taylor, Esq., 55.
Petford, Wm., 73.
Philpott, Kitty, 62.

Pickard, Wm., 30.
Pitt, Eliz., 32.
Placebo, 1, 11.
Platt, Jn., 53.
Polton, Ann, 65.
Pomander, a, 8.
Poole, Dorset, 24.
Poole, Sir Wm., 3.
Populwick, Notts, 64.
Portman, Robt., 24.
Poulton, Ric., 51.
Poundon, Oxon, 28.
Powell, Martha, 22 ; Walt., 31.
Price, Fred., 72 ; Ma., 72 ; Tho., 72.
Prick Song, 7.
Prosser, Jn., 53.
Puckmore, Fra., 21.
Pudsey, 19.
Pulchester, Claus, 67.
Pullett, Martha, 64.
Pulpit Men, 7.
Pultrell, Jn., 3.
Pulvatoft, Tho., 65.
Purfrey, Eliz., 18 ; Ric., 18.
Pyke, Jn., 10.

## Q

Quay, Walt., 17.
Quinney, Eliz., 30.

## R

Radge, Enoch, 66 ; Jn., 66.
Ragsdell, Elean., 55.
Rain of Bwlth, 50.
Rainsbury, Wilts, 52.
Ralf, 20.
Ramsey, Essex, 71.
Rands, Tho., 65.
Rawson, Avery, 1.
Raynsford, Sir Hy., 25.
Rede, Jn., 13.
Rees, Dd., 61.
Reeves, Linst., 58.
Repon, Jn., 3.
Requiem Mass, 1, 11.
Reynolds, Alice, 13 ; Jn., 31 ; Sir Pet., 13 ; Ric., 13.
Ric., Nic., 29.
Richards, Jn., 13 ; Sir Jn., 14.
Richardson, J., 61.
Richmond, York, 66.
Rington, Dorset, 69.
Robin Hood's Bay, York, 71.
Roberts, Gab., 32 ; Ma., 32 ; Phil., 32 ; Tho., 23.

Robinson, Jn., 56 ; Martha, 52.
Rochester, St. Nic., 72.
Rogers, Alice, 29.
Rolles, Poyntz, 23.
Rose, Edw., 49 ; Wm., 51.
Rosterharun, Lois A., 67.
Rowe, Tho., 17.
Rowland, Humph., 19.
Ruddall, Eliz., 66 ; **Wm.**, 66.
Rugby, 63.
Rutland, Tho., 68.
Ryder, 9 ; Jos., 64.
Rye, Sussex, 10, 14, 22, 68.
   Almhouses, 14.
   Middle St., 10.
Rypon, 9.

S

Sadler, Ma., 54 ; Millt., 54.
St. Botolph's, Sussex, 28.
St. Geo., Bloomsbury, 72.
**St.** Geo., Hanover Sq., 71.
St. Giles-in-the-Fields, 70.
St. Mary, Islington, 72.
Sayles, Rob., 9.
Sayley, And., 14.
Scott, Ric., 9.
Secoll, Ric., 14.
Seeley, Wm., 23.
Sellary, Jn., 30.
Senner, Mr., 9.
Sevenhampton, Glouc., 12.
Shavington, Bucks, 64.
Shawe, Jas., 63 ; Martha, 63 ; Rob., 16.
Shene Charterhouse, 7.
Shepherd, Ferd., 32 ; Wm., 3.
Ships—
   Abergavenny, 73.
   Ashia, 70.
   Assistance, 70.
   Capt. Belleisle, 74.
   Centaur, 72.
   Deal Castle, 70.
   Devonshire, 70.
   Dolphin, 39.
   Dominica, 74.
   Dreadnought, 72.
   Duke, 71.
   Fairfax, 70.
   Lyon, 70.
   Marlborough, 55.
   Mediator, 73.
   Nonsuch, 56.
   Norwich, 36.
   Orford, 47.
   Panther, 55.

Ships—*continued*.
   Primrose, 73.
   Resistance, 73.
   Roebuck, 44.
   Royal Sovereign, 71.
   Sunderland, 7.
   Swiftsure, 69, 70.
   Tiger, 40.
   Wager, 42, 44.
   Warwick, 70.
Shorter, Edw., 19.
Shwancenkruge, Jos., 56.
Simeon, Ric., 51.
Simmonds, Lucy, 57.
Simmons, Jerem., 57.
Sir James, 9.
Sleache, Tho., 17.
Slutter, Anne, 29 ; Hest., 29 ; Joan, 29 ; Ma., 29 ; Mercy, 29.
Smith, Abrah., 30 ; Edw., 9, 58 ; Joan, 30 ; Jn., 53 ; Martha, 32 ; Ric., 32 ; Tho., 28, 30 ; Wm., 50.
Sneath, Wm., 51.
Somer, Jn., 10.
Soulderne, Oxon, 23, 69.
Southwark, Borough, 9.
   Guy's Hosp., 73.
   St. Olave, 20-1, 68, 70, 72.
   St. Saviour, 57, 71-2.
Spalding, Linc., 65.
Spencer, 9.
Spry, T., 56.
Stambler, Edm., 15.
Standen, Jn., 22.
Standing Cups, 7.
Stanhurst, Wm., 27.
Stanstead Mountfitchett, Essex, 59, 64.
Staple of Calais, 3.
Stapleton, Ly. Ma., 66 ; Tho., 66.
Starkins, Geo., 59.
Stennynges, 6.
Stepney, Mdx., 22.
Steventon, Beds, 16.
Steward, Tho., 50.
Stildegate, York, 66.
Stocker, Oliver, 58.
Stocks, Jn., 15.
Stondon, Herts, 59, 73.
Stone, Kent, 14, 22.
   And., 56.
Stonebury, Herts, 58-9.
Storkey, Eliz., 13.
Streche, Tho., 3.
Strood, Kent, 7.
Sutton Coldfield, War., 56.
Swallow, Jas., 25.
Swanne, Martha, 22 ; Rob., 22.
Swerston Bridge, 3.

# GENERAL INDEX.

Swinbrook, Oxon, 32.
Sworder, Rose, 63 ; Wm., 58, 63.
Sydenham, Oxon, 28, 65.
Sykes, Rob., 64.
Symms, Edw., 68.
Symonds, Wm., 22.

## T

Tabernacle of our Lady, 8.
Talhurst, Eliz., 22 ; Jerem., 22.
Tayller, Eliz., 15.
Taylor, Benj., 74 ; Eliz., 32 ; Geo., 70, 72 ; Rob., 16.
Taynton, Oxon, 13.
Tempull, 13.
Tenacre, Hy., 7.
Terrolde, Jn., 13.
Thame, 27, 49, 62.
  Chapel, 49.
  Park, 49, 54, 62, 65.
Thomson, Rob., 6.
Thorpe, Edw., 23 ; Jn., 14.
Thurston, Alice, 7 ; Dame Eliz., 6 ; Sir Jn., 6, 9 ; Ric., 9.
Ting, Tho., 70.
Tiplady, Hanh., 66 ; Tho., 66.
Tonbridge, Kent, 14.
Tredway, Jn., 28.
Treffrie, Jn., 18.
Tringham, Tho., 31.
Troute, Edw., 69.
Trowe, Eliz., 25 ; Ric., 25 ; Tho., 25.
Tuam, 27, 31.
Turill, Geo., 70.
Turnour, 12.
Twyford, Bucks, 27-8, 31, 64-5.
Twyselton, 9.
Typlady, Cec., 9 ; Fra., 9 ; Tho., 9-10.
Tyrrell, Ann, 15 ; Tho., 15.
Tythorpe, Oxon, 49, 55.

## U

Uckfield, Sussex, 18.
Ugthorpe, Yorks, 69.
Upton-by-Chalway, 32.
Ursula, 13.

## V

Vanbrough, Eliz., 31 ; Giles, 31 ; Wm., 31.
Vanderbush, Anne, 31 ; Jasp., 31.

Vaughan, Jonas, 50.
Vauxhall, Surrey, 34.
Venell, Mgt., 17.
Verney, Grev., 28, 30.
Vernon, Edw., 49 ; Jn., 49.
Vintners Co., 7.

## W

Wades Mill, Herts. 73.
Wadsworth, Tit., 63.
Waiman, Ric., 70.
Wainman (Waineman), Ann, 65.
  Anth., 69.
  Caroline, 61.
  Christ., 26.
  Denby, 74.
  Elean., 65.
  Eliz., 25, 61, 71-2.
  Sir Fr., 68 ; Fr., 68.
  Geo., 26.
  Hanh., 55.
  Hy., 69.
  Isabel, 70.
  Ja., 55, 66.
  Jn., 25, 64, 72, 74.
  Jos., 70.
  Julia B., 65.
  Maria, 65.
  Ma., 56, 69.
  Mary Ann, 61.
  Oglethorpe, 65.
  Rebecca, 26.
  Ric., 61.
  Ric. B., 61.
  Sar., 64, 69.
  Theod., 64.
  Tho., 64.
  Wm., 26, 56, 65, 66, 69.
Wakefield, 28.
Walham Green, Mdx., 58.
Walker, Rob., 24.
Walton, Wm., 61.
Wannam, Geo., 70.
Wantner, Abel, 24.
Ward, Hy., 58 ; Tho., 19.
Warham, Ellys, 13.
Warner, Jas., 51.
Warwick, Eliz., 75 ; Ric., 59 ; Sar., 75.
Watkins, Jn., 25.
Way, Ric., 49.
Wayman, Alice, 26.
  Ann, 20, 56-7, 72.
  Barth., 20.
  Cassiah, 73.
  Cath., 70.

Wayman—*continued.*
  Daniel, 73.
  Diricus, 68.
  Dorothy, 24.
  Edw., 71
  Eliz., 11, 57, 68, 71, 73.
  Fr., 68.
  Geo., 57, 70, 72.
  Hanh., 67, 73.
  Harrt., 67.
  Hugh, 24.
  Isaac, 53, 72.
  Isab., 71.
  Jerome, 20.
  Joane, 53.
  John, 14, 26, 70, 71-2.
  Jn. Godf., 72.
  Jn. Mich., 72.
  Kath., 69.
  Lewis, 71.
  Lucy, 68.
  Ma., 26, 71-2.
  Mansell, 67.
  Mgt., 16, 26.
  Mark, 56.
  Math., 26.
  Nancy, 56.
  Polly, 56.
  Power, 71.
  Rebecca, 67, 74.
  Ric., 11, 16, 23-4, 70.
  Rob., 26, 68-9, 70, 72.
  Sam., 70.
  Sar., 23, 57.
  Sus., 56, 72.
  Tho., 71.
  Vinc., 26.
  Watson, 55.
  Wm., 11, 71.
Waymand, Dan., 72.
Waymante, Martha, 21.
Waymont, And., 20.
  Mgt., 21.
  Martha, 21.
Wayneman, Christoph., 69.
  Hy., 15, 69.
  Humph., 69.
  Mgt., 69.
  Ma., 69.
  Nic., 15.
  Sar., 69.
  Tho., 69.
  Wm., 26, 28, 69.
Weaman, Ann, 27, 30, 49.
  Dor., 56.
  Elean., 27.
  Eliz., 27, 30-1.
  Greg., 27, 30.
  Hy., 27.

Weaman—*continued.*
  Jn., 27, 30.
  Ma., 27, 30, 49.
  Ric., 27.
  Tho., 30, 49.
  Wm., 27, 30-1.
Weavour, Alice, 24 ; Jas., 24.
Webbe, 13.
Webster, Joane, 24.
Weiman, Henr., 16-7.
Wellingborough, 70.
Wells, Rob., 17.
Welyms, Jn., 2-3.
Wenman, Alice, 2.
  Amos, 52.
  Ann, 2, 12-3, 25, 29, 52, 60, 70, 74.
  Charlotte, 60.
  Chas., 52-3, 60, 73.
  Doralissa, 32.
  Dor., 19, 30.
  Eadey, 51.
  Elean., Lady, 65-6.
  Eliz., 12-3, 17-8, 52-3, 60.
  Ellen, 16.
  Emote, 2.
  Ferd., 28.
  Fras., 17-8, 27 ; Sir Fr., 25, 29.
  Frances, 17.
  Geo., 71.
  Giles, 17.
  Hy., 12-3, 52.
  Herb. Hy., 49.
  Isab., 18.
  Ja., 19, 68.
  Janet, 62, 73.
  Jn., 50, 52-3, 68.
  Jos., 50-1, 60.
  Kath., 31.
  Ld., 71.
  Mgy., 18, 68.
  Ma., 28, 30—2, 49, 51, 54.
  Martha, 52, 70, 72.
  Phil., 27, 30, 32.
  Phil., Lord, 49, 54-5, 62, 64.
  Ric., Lord, 31.
    Sir, 10, 12-3, 17—19, 23, 28-9, 49, 52, 54, 62, 69, 70, 71, 73.
    Hon., 62, 65.
  Ric. Hy., 60.
  Rob., 29.
  Sam., 25.
  Sar., 51-3, 72.
  Sophia, 49, 54.
  Sus., 49, 52-3.
  Tho., 2, 12-3, 19, 23, 68-9, 72.
    Sir, 27.
  Tho. Fr., 49, 54, 61.
  Wm., 12-3, 16-7, 70-1.

## GENERAL INDEX.

West., Sam., 62.
Westminster, 51, 71.
  St. Margt., 20, 71.
Weston, Wm., 61.
Weston, Radn., 50.
Westweld, Oxon, 2.
Weyman, Eliz., 56.
  Fr., 68.
  Gerard, 31.
  Is., 70.
  Jacob, 71.
  Jerem., 23.
  Jn., 50, 56, 69.
  Ju. Mich., 72.
  Josea, 23.
  Judith, 70-1.
  Juliana, 68.
  Morris, 69.
  Pethia, 69.
  Sar., 70.
  Tho., 50, 69.
  Walt., 70.
  Wm., 50.
Weymond, Edw., 69 ; Jn., 73.
Weymouth, 72.
Whalley, Rob., 49.
Whayman, Cath., 67.
  Edw., 67.
  Oliver, 72.
  Tho., 70.
  Wm., 72.
Whaymand, Jn., 55.
Wheigham, Oliv., 27 ; Wm., 27.
Wheler, Jn., 2.
Whinchelsea, 22.
White, 8 ; Rob., 10.
White Waltham, Berks, 52.
Whitechapel, 71.
White Cross St., Mdx., 66.
Whiting, Sir Jn., 2-3.
Whitney (Witney), Oxon, 2, 10—13, 25, 30, 32, 49, 64-5.
  Chapel, 12.
  Park, 12, 69.
Wickenstill, Lanc., 65.
Wickstead, Jn. Churchill, 49.
Wildegoose, Izaard, 65.
Willes, Wm., 61.
Williams, Edw., 62 ; Howell, 56.
Wilson, Rob., 21-2.
Windey, Jas., 62 ; Math., 62.
Windsor, 60.
Winter, Sus., 17.
Wisbeach, 65.
Withabed, Jn., 61.
Witnesham, Suff., 14.
Wood, Edmd., 18 ; Wm., 53.
Woodcocke, Tho., 24.
Worley, 9.

Worshopp, Jn., 9.
Wright, Tho., 14.
Wroughton, Phil., 64.
Wykeham, Harrt., 54-5, 62.
  Phil., 54-5.
  Phil. Tho., 65.
  Soph., 54-5.
  Wm., 62.
  Wm. Ric., 65.
Wylshyr, Xfer, 16.
Wyman, Alice, 23.
  Ann, 57, 73.
  Cath., 58.
  Christopher, 58.
  Eliz., 19, 23, 53, 57, 58-9, 63-4, 71.
  Fanny, 63-4.
  Fr., 24, 58-9, 63-4.
  Fr. Jn., 59.
  Geo., 21, 58-9.
  Hy., 32.
  Jas., 73.
  Joan, 21.
  Jn., 19, 21, 24, 32, 53, 57-8, 70.
  Joseph, 53, 58, 73.
  Julyan, 23.
  Kath., 63-4.
  Lauretta, 21.
  Mgt., 17-8, 23-4, 57.
  Martha, 32.
  Ma., 59, 70-1.
  Math., 57.
  Phœbe, 19.
  Rebecca, 23.
  Ric., 21, 59, 63.
  Rob., 17, 22, 32.
  Rose, 58, 63-4.
  Sar., 57, 73.
  Tho., 21, 58, 73.
  Wm., 17, 21, 24, 63, 65.
Wymant, And., 68 ; Martha, 68.
Wyment, Cath., 51.
  Eliz., 51.
  Ma., 51.
  Sam., 51.
  Sar., 51.
Wymonde, Alice, 10.
  Agn., 10.
  Anne, 22.
  Bridg., 10, 22.
  Dor., 68.
  Eliz., 1, 22.
  Fr., 14.
  Geo., 22.
  Joane, 1, 10, 14, 68.
  Jn., 10, 14, 18, 68-9.
  Lowdye, 18.
  Mawde, 3.
  Paul, 14, 22.
  Ric., 3, 10.

Wymonde—*continued*.
  Rob., 3, 10.
  Sybil, 22.
  Tho., 6, 7, 18, 69.
  Wm., 10, 14, 22, 68.
Wynman, Emm., 2.
  Jn., 2.
  Ric., 2.

Y

Yate, Leon., 14.
Year's Mind, The, 13.
Yette, 13.
Yonge, Dr., 3 ; Tho., 9.
York, 69.